GREEN GARDENER .

Green Gardener

How an Amateur Created a Wild Garden

BETTY DOUGHERTY

line illustrations by the author

DAVID & CHARLES

NEWTON ABBOT   LONDON
NORTH POMFRET (VT)   VANCOUVER

ISBN 0 7153 6498 7
Library of Congress Catalog Card Number 74-81054
© Betty Dougherty 1975

Set in 11 on 13pt Baskerville and printed in
Great Britain by Compton Printing Ltd Aylesbury
for David & Charles (Holdings) Limited
South Devon House Newton Abbot Devon

Published in the United States of America
by David & Charles Inc North Pomfret
Vermont 05053 USA

Published in Canada by Douglas David &
Charles Limited 3645 McKechnie Drive
West Vancouver BC

Contents

List of Plates

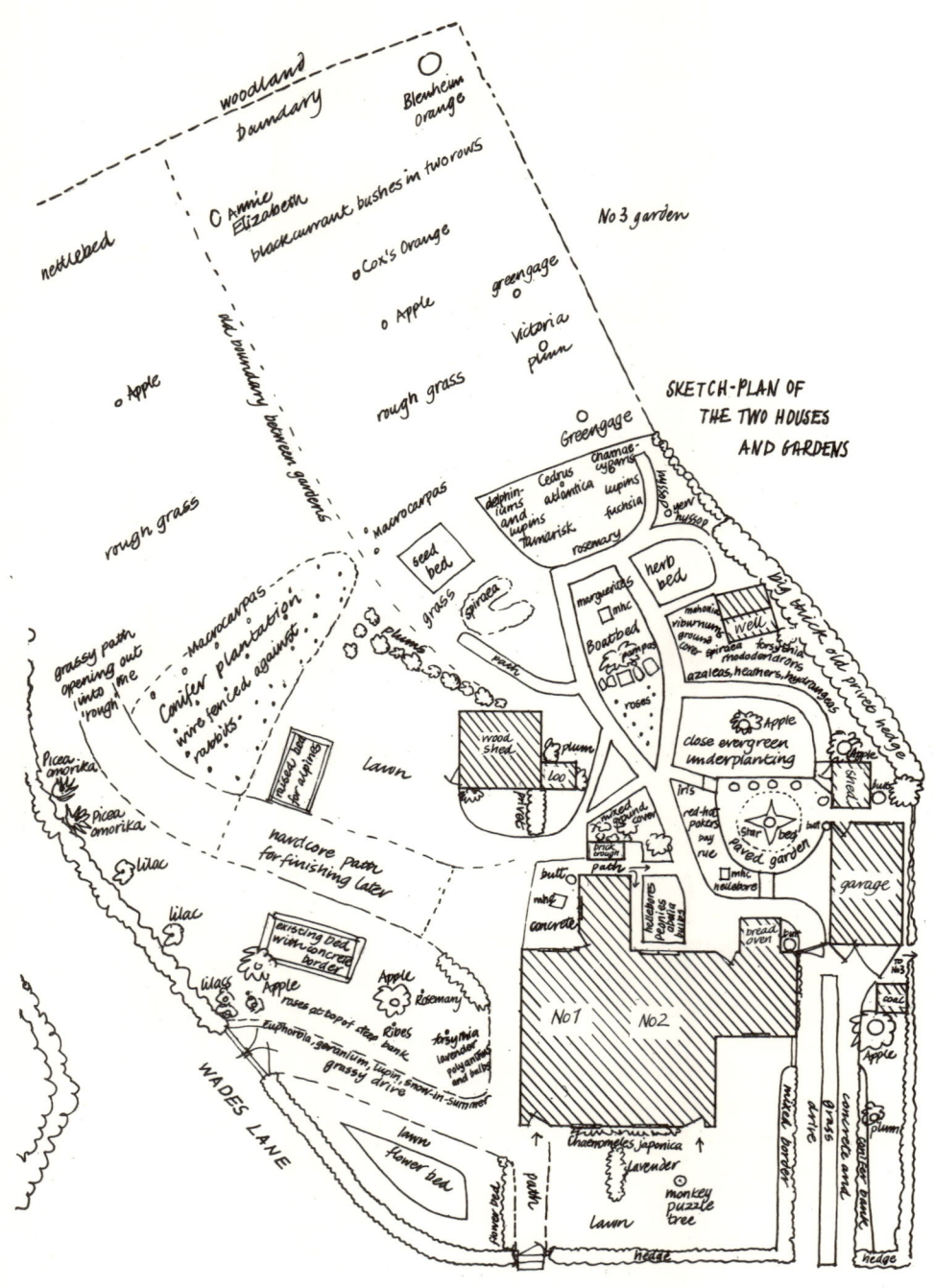

woodland boundary

Blenheim orange ○

No 3 garden

nettlebed

Annie ○
Elizabeth

blackcurrant bushes in two rows

○ Cox's Orange

○ Apple   greengage

Victoria ○
plum

rough grass

○ Apple

rough grass

old boundary between gardens

Greengage ○

SKETCH-PLAN OF
THE TWO HOUSES
AND GARDENS

○ Macrocarpas

grass

seed
bed

delphin-
iums
and
lupins

Cedrus
atlantica

chamae-
cyparis

lupins

fuchsia

festum

open
hedge

Tamarisk

rosemary

marguerites

herb
bed

magnolia
viburnum
ground
cover

Macrocarpas

Conifer plantation
wire fenced against
rabbits

plums

spiraea

mhc

Boxbed

spiraea

azaleas, heathers, hydrangeas

well

big thick old privet hedge

path

roses

3 Apple

close evergreen
underplanting

Apple

shed

grassy path
opening out
into the
rough

raised bed
for saving

lawn

wood
shed

plum

loo

beans

iris

red-hot
pokers

ground cover

star
bed

big
bell

Apple

hellebore

Picea
omorika

Picea
omorika

hardcore path
for finishing later

mixed ground cover

brick
trough

paved garden

mhc
hellebore

garage

lilac

path

bush

holleborus Peonies
Pinks
Lilies

concrete

bread
oven

to
No3

lilac

existing bed
with concrete
border

Apple

Apple

Rosemary

mhc

concrete

lilacs

roses at top of steep
bank

Ribes

forsythia
lavender
polyanthus
and bulbs

No 1

No 2

goal

WADES LANE

Euphorbia, geranium, lupin, snow-in-summer
grassy drive

lawn
flower bed

Chaemomeles japonica

lavender

monkey
puzzle
tree

lawn

mixed border

concrete and
grass drive

Apple

plum

hedge

hedge

Introduction

THIS is a book about an escape to freedom; escape, not in the prisoner-of-war sense, but from the pressures of life to a small house and a large garden in Suffolk. It is about their acquisition by a middle-aged single woman with very slender resources, making the most of mortgages, grants and loans to secure a resting place for the remainder of her working life, and a place for retirement later.

As you may guess from the title, it is chiefly about the garden —an unwanted incidental at first; about the therapeutic value of gardening, especially of weeding; the excitement of finding out, first, what plants the garden already contained, and second, what plants to buy, on either aesthetical or practical grounds; about what to avoid and what to look for.

So far, there seems to be no book for the extreme amateur (one who could put a row of potatoes between two rows of raspberries without thinking about the effect on the shallow roots of the latter when it came to earthing up the potatoes, and one who had not realised that there was such a thing as grey foliage). Taking the bull by the horns then—'grasping the nettle' might be more appropriate—I have set out in this book my own experiences with plants for the benefit of other green gardeners.

The book describes, too, the subsequent acquisition of the other half of the semi-detached house and the welding together of the two gardens, which had previously been barricaded apart to keep out the next-door cats which bred like rabbits and spoiled all the best plants. The overstocking of the first garden and the newly won knowledge of the growing potential of selected items on a particular soil under specific climatic conditions, gave me the opportunity of planning with known factors. By observation of height and growth rate (I had previously been merely a dis-interested and therefore casual observer of plants), and by experience of new plants within the context of the 'residents', a wilderness has become a wild garden. This knowledge is basic, but often under-emphasised by specialists, professionals and other enthusiasts, who seem to expect one to know by instinct how to proceed.

Years have sped by with not a moment wasted, and at the end of it all—well, there *is* no end, for the fascination and scope for improvement is still boundless. All one needs is time and energy.

Chapter 1

Finding the House

LIFE has some curious quirks. 'There, but for the Grace of God, I go' can become 'There, thank God, I go', but the reasons for either state can never be fully understood when one looks back over the events preceding a particular episode in life, and so it was with me.

Recovering from the state of depression in which major surgery often leaves one, I received warmly an invitation to stay with Naomi and Bryan at their house in Dorset. That first country weekend was a revelation, never to be forgotten, because from that stems all my present happiness. It was not that I had never been to the country before, but previously there had always been some obligation, some tie to hamper movement and to prevent me from doing what I knew I should be doing with my life, enough to make me feel in a state of rebellion against it all. But here was the perfect, homely hospitality, nothing formal; a warmth of feeling in the village pub on Sunday morning, lungs full of good fresh air, and at night after a splendid meal (which only those who live alone can appreciate), a blissful, drowsy comfort ending in unaided sleep.

No obligations towards one's undemanding host and hostess— complete freedom, and in such delightful surroundings. These too were part of the cure: sunshine, wind in the face (previously I had cringed and covered up from the sun, as one does who

burns but does not tan), the deep colour of the sea in the distance
beyond the hills, pleasant company and similar tastes, and a deep
understanding of which at that time I was only dimly aware.
But most of all, freedom.

During holidays spent in the countryside there had always
been a tremendous urge to live in such surroundings, among
people as yet little affected by the so-called 'civilisation' of city
life, people who still find time to stand and stare and evaluate.
Applying for a job in Torquay, I was discouraged to find what
comparatively low rates of pay and poor working conditions
existed out of London. So the thought was in my mind of finding
a little resting-place somewhere where it would be possible to
arrive and leave at will. Since I had scarcely any working capital
to show after twenty years' work, it had to be something modest.
On a visit to Bath, I went out to see a converted stable. There
were disadvantages, not the least of which was that no source
of money approached would have anything to do with a mortgage
on a converted stable without a damp-proof course. From that
holiday I returned disconsolate but still determined to go on
looking, and alerted my friends as well.

Bryan, painting in Suffolk, telephoned one July day to suggest
looking at several likely places of which he had obtained parti-
culars and keys. I travelled not very hopefully, as I had never
been to Suffolk before and imagined it quite flat with a few
scrubby trees and miles and miles of uninterrupted fields.
Education in that respect began on the journey towards Hadleigh,
and was further continued the next day as we began our rounds
of the houses he had spotted.

Several were Tudor-old, with massive beams full of woodworm,
sloping floors in the bedrooms, where the weight of the over-
hanging upper storey was too much for foundations in light sandy
soil, and walls of broken lath-and-plaster between timber framing.
They were in a deplorable state, but as there was very little
purchase money available, I had not expected a palace. Cun-

ningly, Bryan withheld until the last a little semi-detached slate and brick farm-worker's cottage three miles out of Hadleigh. As we drove towards it, he indicated it and I said, 'What, that!' in my most diplomatic and endearing way. He overlooked such rudeness and merely said, 'Wait until you see the view from the window.'

He was right: from that moment nowhere else would do. It was even called 'Mount Pleasant'. There was the landscape spread out before me; behind was the sheltering hillside, and only three other houses—the other half of 'mine' and another pair. Unpromising as that first sight of the house had been, there were so many compensations that it faded into insignificance. The windows were generously proportioned (as were the draughts they admitted during the first winter there) and the rooms, although small, were quite large enough to keep clean and tidy in the weekends ahead.

The cottage was far more than I expected to pay, but I was so enthralled that every energy was bent towards its acquisition, and there were many tense moments when I thought it was 'in the bag', only to find that some other bit of legal fiddle-de-dee was likely to allow some rotten outsider to filch it from me. No mother fought harder for the welfare of her child than I did to get a foothold inside that little house—no thought for the garden then, you see.

It was without proper sanitation and with only one cold-water tap, but an improvement grant from the local council took care of that. Of course there were snags. The house was Victorian, and I am a middle-aged, single woman—never a good prospect for a mortgage. One has to 'own' the house before a grant is allowed, and it has to be sound enough structurally to warrant improvement. There has to be sufficient ground in a suitable position to put in a septic-tank drainage system in accordance with the local bye-laws, so a valuer and surveyor came, and to be on the safe side, I engaged a local solicitor to look after the points which could not be dealt with by remote control from London.

On completion I was horrified at my temerity, for how was the house to be furnished, with all those bills to pay for proper plumbing, hot water and repairs? The extravagant habit of buying a pair of shoes when I saw some I liked would have to go. I was overweight so it would pay me in more ways than one to eat and drink less. When expenditure on whims like nice books and beautiful pottery was added up, I was abashed. If I wanted that house, I would have to take a big tuck in myself.

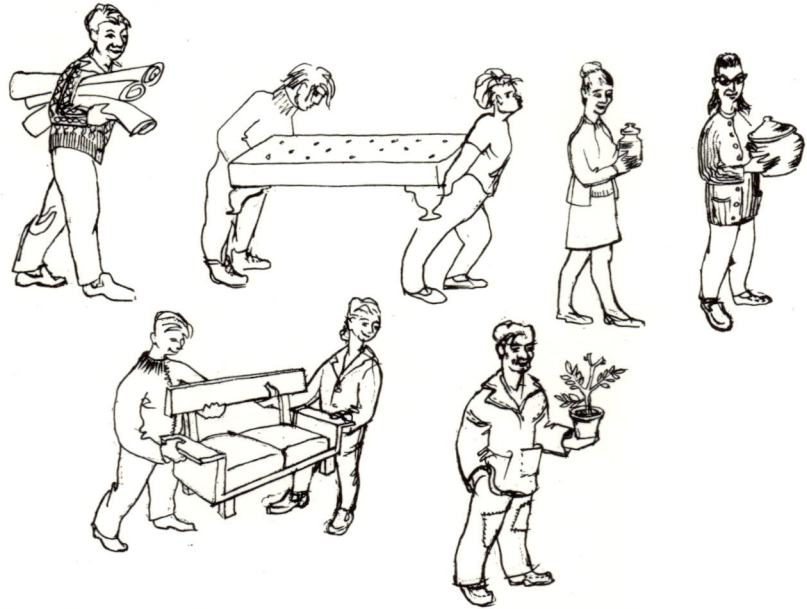

In hospital I had marvelled at my friends' kindness in so constantly coming to see me, always bringing some little present. Now they proved as faithful again, with offers of carpets, furniture and all sorts of things which fitted so well into hastily devised decorating schemes that I could scarcely have chosen better.

Some of the carpet offcuts, given with a 'don't-know-what-you-can-do-with-it, but-it's-only-lying-about-here-gathering-dust' shrug of the shoulders, were very useful. The most delightful of these offerings was a strip of bright red about 18in wide which still greets guests as they come into the house by the back door, and calls forth the obvious comment which starts the flow of conversation.

Then there were the exciting expeditions to local junk shops, from which came a handsome old wooden armchair and one or two other useful objects for house and garden. Other outings met with equal success: a neat little basket chair found in Wickham Market; much later, a well-cared-for mahogany chest of drawers, all glowing, from Debenham; garden chairs; and even a wheelbarrow which surprisingly had to have its wheel removed before it could be fitted into the car beside Father. Life was fascinating. No time for brooding or feeling sorry for myself. My friends grinned and kept me at it.

Even in the first rapture about the view from the window in the front of the house, I had noticed its terrible state of dilapidation. Still, this was not a deterrent because I have always done my own painting and decorating and this was just about my size of house. The ceilings are low by some standards but right in relation to the room sizes. By standing on a chair or a stool I can reach the ceilings, and that is to me a comfortable decorating height.

One day a friend asked whether she could come and see the house. 'As soon as it is in working order,' I replied, thinking of all the old bits of lino, spiders' webs, mouse holes and other drawbacks to being a good hostess. Besides, Maureen had lent a sympathetic ear to my no-doubt-boring enthusiasm about the house, and I felt that she deserved a look.

'Ian and I would love to help you, if you like,' she said; and this was the first and most valuable of many kindnesses shown by friends when they knew that I had my foot inside my own front door at last. After living in a rented flat for most of my adult life, the incentive offered by home ownership is almost a tangible force, but I was astonished that others should be so willing to lend a hand at hard, grubby work.

The spiders were our greatest hate, Maureen's and mine. Either Ian was indifferent or felt that it was beneath a man's dignity to admit to not liking them, but there were many webs

and scores of dead bluebottles on the window ledges. Visiting the loo was the worst ordeal. It wasn't that it smelt all that bad, especially when the bucket had been emptied at the top of the garden and some fresh Elsan Blue put into it. It was the spiders. The shed was falling apart at the seams, and a large virginia creeper which covered the outside had sent exploratory tendrils into the interior. Entering with a torch at night, ensuring that there were no spiders in the way, and then turning round to look at the other side of the shed, only to feel something tickling the back of one's neck, was far from funny. With a shriek, and probably on occasions with our pants down, Maureen or I would erupt from The Residence swearing to endure agonies rather than go in there again.

One of the nicest things about coming to the house was to be able to leave the car unlocked in the drive, and the door to the house unlocked at night, without the thought of someone lurking about ready to pinch the car, or one of its new tyres, or to syphon off some petrol. And until the local bobby scared me out of my wits by banging on the back door to say that the car was parked in the road without lights, the back door was always unlocked.

At this stage I was set on a course of intensive weekending, right through the winter, preparing for summer guests again, but under better circumstances. The builders began their activeties about the beginning of winter, with instructions to leave water, light and Calor gas in a state for my use on arrival on Friday evenings. My most hideous nightmare at that time was of arriving late at night to find all the pipes frozen, or the electricity cut off because they were in the middle of a job and of their packing up and leaving as it was 5.30 pm, or the Calor gas all used up—or all three. But then I did not know my Suffolk men. Not only do they not have that 'Down tools, men, it's 5.30' attitude to the job, but they completed it in a couple of months where it would have taken a London builder twice that time because he would be going off on another job to keep that 'on the boil' and the owner satisfied. If these chaps did have another job, mine did not suffer from it.

The only time missed from visiting the house that year was after snow had fallen all week, and all day on the Friday without stopping, so that after three hours of skidding and sliding to Romford, it was obvious that it would be foolish to carry on. All that weekend I worried about the roof. Were the slates coming off in the high winds? Had the wet seeped through and made big wet patches on the ceiling, or worse still, dripped whitewash and snow on to my new bed covers? I was Frenzy-of-Inactivity personified.

Some years later, following two personal tragedies, history was to repeat itself, and Mount Pleasant came again to the rescue of sanity by providing an overwhelming demand for work in both house and garden, requiring careful timing and organisation. A veritable godsend.

Chapter 2

Discovering the Garden

SO far I had been busy with the painting and decorating but the day came when the garden could no longer be ignored. Oddly enough I remember neither the occasion nor the reason for the decision that it was time to tidy it up a bit. Perhaps it was the evening on which I arrived hot and tired from a gruelling day at the office and a sticky drive up from London in the Friday evening traffic jams, to find that my kind neighbour, Basil Keeble, had cut the front grass and the hedge. What a difference that 'haircut' made. A flower border was actually uncovered beside the grassy driveway.

At the back, the garden was a shambles where the builders had been digging trenches for the septic-tank installation. A charming well with a wooden roof stood off from the house, and I was told that only a few years before, all four houses in the row used it. 'Forty turns down and forty up,' my neighbour Betty said, 'and we often used to lose a bucket down there and spend hours fishing for it. We all used to gather for a chat there—at that time the other houses were occupied by family. There were five children about, and everyone seemed ever so happy in those days, laughing and talking across the gardens.'

'Pails stood about in the kitchens, and we had a man from the council to test the water regularly. One day he said it wasn't fit to drink, so we all had to go to Fox Farm for it, three-quarters of a mile away, with an uphill walk back with the pails of water. The mains water was only put in about 1961.' But everyone was 'ever so happy'.

I had been looking forward to friends' children listening to the plop of stones falling into the water so far below. To my dismay, going to drop a stone in myself—we never grow up—there was a flat 'bat' from below; the wretched builders had put the soil from the trenches down the well to get rid of it, and from the sound of it, some concrete too. Miserably I concluded that they had had their instructions from the council to make the well unusable, in case of pollution from the septic-tank drainage. Little did I think that it was the *topsoil* as well as the well's own charm which had been sacrificed. In those days topsoil meant nothing to me.

I seem to remember that it was beans I wanted. Runner beans, lots and lots of them. And then there was the fruit: apples, plums, greengages, raspberries, blackcurrants, redcurrants, gooseberries —all buried in a dense jungle of weeds and the most enormous nettles. It is said that soil on which nettles have grown is very fertile; all I knew about it then was that they stung very badly every time I ventured near those luscious blackcurrants which yielded so well after two years' neglect. So the war on nettles began at the top of the 160ft plot—and top it certainly was, a good uphill drag with tools or water, or even just oneself.

At the same time, because of the drainage system, a rough plan had already emerged for the lower garden near the house. Before the builders started in November, a huge fuchsia bush was moved from the path of their trench. It was a major under-taking, as the roots were enormous and very deep, a product, as I now know, of the sandy dryness to which the garden reverts in summer. It is a wonder to me now that the fuchsia is still alive, as my strength and patience gave out and the poor thing was wrested from the ground. A few roots were broken, but luckily the fine soil allows deep-rooted things to be pulled up without

too much harm. To get the bush up the garden away from the probable line of the 'works' was another tussle, as it was far too heavy for one person and there was no wheelbarrow—well, I wasn't a gardener yet, was I? So it was towed as far away as possible and roughly bedded down. No such *finesse* as heeling in. As it was early winter, perhaps it was lucky enough to get some rain quite soon after the ordeal. Certainly I gave it no further thought.

A lovely red rose, still in bloom, stood just where the plans showed the site of the first manhole cover. Glancing round and seeing a piece of ground without much plant life showing, I dug a hole, uprooted the rose with the same casual treatment as before, and stuffed it in. There it stayed outside the dining-room window blooming its way happily into December until a particularly hard frost finished off the last buds. Four years later it was moved again but is still going strong. Its name is still a mystery, but who cares? It grows and prospers and that is enough.

In the spring and early summer I took a closer look around the garden, partly to see whether the fuchsia had survived. It was not to be seen. But there were exciting signs of life in other things: crocuses, snowdrops, daffodils, the lovely bright magenta primula, 'Wanda' (though I didn't know its name until three years later), in profusion along the edges of paths and here and there in the hinterland. Star of Bethlehem had me guessing for a long time, and my patient friend at the office, Evelyn Prideaux, who was beseiged with questions during that first year in the garden, provided the answer. She and others also provided many of the plants which are only now reaching maturity.

Philadelphus—ignorantly I called it syringa at that time—was another bonus from the previous occupant. In that first June, it sent its beautiful odour across the garden in the evening to reach me at the back door as I put my head out to say goodnight to the garden. Significantly it grew beside the outside privy, and I noticed that the privy next door had a great bush of it too!

You may think it crazy, but I have always said goodbye to the house on leaving it at weekends, and greeted it on arrival, caressing it with my mind on both occasions; and it seemed natural to do the same with the garden. Having planted or moved something the week before, the first act on entering the garden, even in winter by torchlight, is to go and see whether the patient is all right, and to finger it and murmur encouragement or congratu-

lations as appropriate. Often I wondered whether the neighbours, especially the 'attached' ones, could see and hear me, and think I was half-witted. But it did not matter to me what they were thinking, as these were my plants in my garden. What is more, many other gardeners have said that plants respond to this interest in their welfare. Several of which I have despaired have risen almost from the dead—which brings me back to the fuchsia. It did just that.

Of course I was looking for it not only at the wrong time of year but in a landscape made unfamiliar by the builders' work. The whole garden seemed to consist of a rather dreary uphill slope of yellowish soil which was mainly gravel and sandy subsoil, and the well was really the only landmark. The fuchsia had been beyond the well, I thought, but only tall grass grew there now. No branches reached 6ft to the sky. Probably I stood mourning on the very spot where it was struggling to its feet. Later that year it was astonishing to find a whole run of fresh new fuchsia shoots in that area, and after poking about a bit, weeding round them to give them breathing and feeding space, it became evident that the high winds to which the garden is prone had 'proned' the fuchsia and it was shooting now from a recumbent position, very effectively too. It is now in girth the same-sized bush which was moved originally, but rather shorter, no doubt because it is in a less sheltered position than before. Much later in my gardening education, I learned that this is one way some shrubs reestablish after becoming too woody, when limbs get broken down and reroot at the point of contact with the earth.

Another great joy found prospering quietly in a corner was the rose 'Mermaid', with glossy leaves, and growth so riotous as to be classed as rampant. It is situated not far from a beautiful late-flowering honeysuckle which climbs along one side of the garage, while 'Mermaid' climbs along a rustic wood structure set at an angle towards the end of the shed and of the honeysuckle. When the two protagonists meet, what will happen? I have read somewhere that a mermaid does not like her fins clipped, so perhaps the honeysuckle should be pruned away. I don't feel like taking a hand—it seems too umpire-like.

When the builders had gone, the first and most obvious thing to be done was to disguise the manhole covers, but in such a way that they would be easily available for inspection of the drainage if necessary. Nasturtiums, I thought. Quick and easy and don't need attention. Lovely colours. Brighten up the place a bit. Needs it.

Seed was sown and in due course the flowers came and so did the blackfly. They were too near the house for my liking, so off to the bonfire went the nasturtiums, blackfly and all. They had, after all, been blooming for some while and had gone a bit straggly. Their planting started me off cultivating the patch outside the back door. This was logical because it was the part of the garden which would be seen every time anyone came in and out—the milkman, the neighbours, visitors, me. Digging as I thought in the approved manner, deeply (not double digging or any of that malarky, just a forkful at a time to get the weeds out), brick after brick appeared, and enough stones to fill a beach. In fact I began to wonder whether I was busy undoing what the builders had just put there as drainage. Then a piece or two of crazy paving came up with the earth. All these finds had been at the same level, about 10in below the surface. As I plodded on, the pile of hardware grew. Glancing at the little paved pathway to the old loo a short distance away, it slowly dawned on me that under all that depth of earth between me and that path was probably a paved garden. Then I knew what an archaeologist must feel like when he knows he's on to something big like a Roman mosaic pavement. My 'Roman mosaic' was *far* more valuable at that moment. It would alter the whole concept of that area of the garden—regardless of the fact that up until that moment there was no concept in mind.

Digging away frenziedly, not bothering so much now to get every single weed out, but concentrating on my find, I wondered how best to make use of it in relation to the rest of the area taking shape around the paths trodden into the gravelly soil either side of the trench, which had stretched 40ft up the garden slope from the house. There was a short piece of concrete path leading up from the back door to join the lower end of the 'sheep track', and a bed had been planned already between the two branches of this path. What should be done now?

The paved area grew, and at first it took on a very curious

apple tree

privet hedge

forsythia

philadelphus

primula 'Wanda'

back door here   bread oven here

shape in relation to the pathway to the loo. This curved away from the house, while the far edge of the paving opposite to it seemed to come into two little bumps like a baby's bottom. Along the side furthest from the house was a retaining wall for what I now call rather grandly 'The Terrace Bed'. In the centre of this bed was an apple tree, with another not far away on the right. In front of the retaining wall was a wide strip of concrete path before the paving started towards the house. Two paths led out of this, very oddly. Eventually I decided that there had to be a central point and when a suitable gap appeared in the paving, that was it. A pygmy rose of deep velvety-red from Woolworth's was planted there and my day was made.

There seemed to be a great deal of coal in the soil under the paving, and very likely the rose did not care for this diet, for it died after one glamorous season. It was replaced by fuchsias with mammoth blooms, also from Woolworth's, and not looking a bit like the picture on the bag. The centre bed was now enlarged to a star shape. Later on I had to rehabilitate this because of overgrowth. It is a point worth noting that if you make formal shaped beds, you must be prepared to keep them tidy.

About this time a diary was kept regularly for the first time in my life, about the developments in house and garden, but especially the garden. Entered religiously every weekend, typed up during the following week and any necessary plans or diagrams added, the whole project was kept under review and ideas sprang up in abundance. Little did I foresee the future value of this. It enabled me to compare from one year to the next the performance of a favourite plant, or to look up when it was acquired, or where planted (*very* important, as you will see later).

There was plenty of fruit during that first year—quite unexpected since I had done nothing to promote it. Victoria plums headed the list with over a 70lb yield from two trees. Earl River gave only 3lb but my fruit-farmer neighbour said they were often 'a bit shy'. Later the tree succumbed to gale-force winds. It was already a fantastic shape because of these.

I had been looking forward to the greengages but they only produced one miserable pound from two trees—perhaps they were even more shy. Only 4½lb of apples have been recorded though I know that there were hundreds more but not worth eating. It has been noticeable that since the weeds have been cleared away from under and around the big Anne Elizabeth and the Blenheim Orange at the top of the garden, the apples have been bigger and of better quality. That first year they were spotty and scabby and fit only for composting.

The blackcurrants did well but more netting was clearly needed to keep off the birds. Redcurrants and raspberries seem to have stuck at 2lb each, but again in later years have been more productive because they have been better treated. What joy, though, to take one's guests out in the early morning to gather their breakfast raspberries themselves, and to send them off with carrier bags full of plums. Even bottled fruit made acceptable Christmas presents when all my friends knew how stretched I was for money.

Chapter 3

Weeds: to Kill or Cure?

BY June that year most of the lower garden was cleared of weeds, or at least, those that showed. It was time to pay attention to the great nettle beds at the top end of the garden. I called on friends at Basingstoke one day and mentioned the size of the problem. Without hesitation Leslie said, 'If you can put up with us for a weekend, I'll bring a drum of paraquat and spray them for you.' Such a magnificent offer was more than I dared hope for, so it was snapped up with a note in our diaries straight away. Once more the sketch map was produced, handed out to all visitors because the house is right off the beaten track.

Even Leslie was daunted by the sight of those nettles. I had had a go at cutting them down with a reap hook, losing my way among their 5ft stems, and cutting a wide pathway in a round-about way from one side of the garden to the other. It was rather like a maze. Leslie donned his spraying garb, an old mackintosh and gum boots, and set to work. By the end of a long, hot day those nettles looked rather sorry for themselves, but as he pointed out, to be really effective the paraquat should be used again in three days' time. Anyway, it made a start to the war, which was later carried on more easily for the paraquat, by uprooting the majority. This may appear to be a duplication of effort, since paraquat is usually just left to kill the plants off. Those nettles were far too tough for that, and the spray had played its part by

a path through the nettles

acting as a deterrent to growth, making it all much easier to deal with later. The fine, sandy soil helped too, except that the roots were some 8 to 9ft long, and near the leaves, almost 1in in diameter. No doubt they were the better for the contents of the Elsan bucket, for there seemed to be no other means of disposal of this. The oak and beech wood behind the garden would also have provided valuable food.

It is difficult to describe the staisfaction to be had from getting out those nettles. At first I put it down to the easiness of the soil, but later, stretching a weary body in bed, I realised that there was a compulsiveness about it. Times for eating became more and more erratic, until it was a case of snatching an orange or a glass of milk when too tired to pull another root.

But what a joy when the area was tamed and found to contain many more gooseberry bushes, some more raspberries and a huge blackberry bramble. This had made its way in from the wood, but it seemed possible that by careful pruning and tying up, I

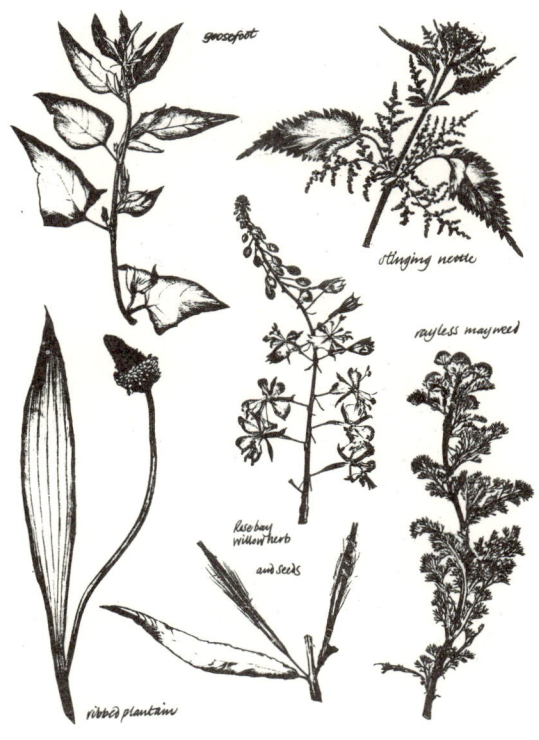

might get some good fruit. I had reckoned without the birds, but did not begrudge them their juicy morsels as there was so much of everything else. I like to feel that they were grateful and so did not attack the raspberry patch near the house, from which each year I have such a delicious and prolific crop.

That big job of weeding came at a time when I was most depressed and anti-social. I shall always maintain that it saved my sanity by getting out of my system all the evil, destructive

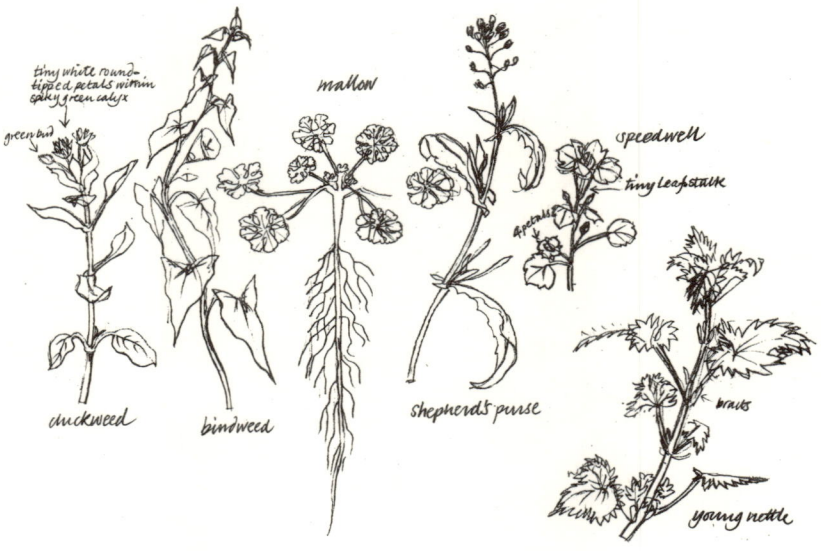

tiny white round-tipped petals within spiky green calyx

green bud

mallow

speedwell

tiny leafstalk

duckweed

bindweed

shepherd's purse

nettle

young nettle

feelings, and at the same time showing something constructive in return. I still find that pulling out the odd tuft of grass, or dealing with an encroaching patch of speedwell or shepherd's purse, holds the same bonus of satisfaction and cleansing. Weeding can be thoroughly recommended for its therapeutic value, and gardening in general too, as shown in a publication for the Disabled Living Foundation, called *The Easy Path to Gardening*.

For one thing it is a great advantage to be far enough away

from other people to be able to talk to yourself, or to turn over in the mind the current problem in a peaceful environment—or to abandon that in favour of philosophising on life in general. So many things fall into perspective while digging, weeding, planting out or mowing the grass. Even figures of speech mean more. 'Cropping up', for example, must surely have had its roots in the soil. Unearthing some weird-looking iron cooking pots and other domestic china utensils, I began to see where the American expression 'dig that crazy . . . whatever-it-is' might have started. A 'pot shot' might easily be the poacher's shot at game destined for his cooking pot—and could a 'grass widow' possibly be a woman left high and dry by a husband playing with his new ride-on mower?

Since Nature abhors a vacuum, something had to be planted quickly to take the place of the weeds which had been eradicated, especially in the beds near the house. I am ashamed to say that it did not occur to me before filling those beds that this was just the right opportunity to alter things round. That bed outside the dining-room window, which later had to be reduced in size to move the soil away from the house walls, could have been dealt with earlier, so saving a lot of the damp in the house. But reading about ground cover and discovering the value of peat, diverted by a newly found interest in plants grown for their foliage effects, others for their textures and yet others to keep the weeds from growing, I was well on the road to ruin. Not that peat costs much; in fact, in view of its many advantages it still seems to be a great bargain when bought in the larger pack sizes. Not only will it recondition soil, breaking down clay and leavening sandy soil with organic matter, but it provides a longer period of moisture retention for the plants it surrounds. Any weeds left growing in the ground will thrust up through it in time, so they must all be extracted with their roots, before applying at least a 2in layer of wetted peat on top of thoroughly watered ground, to prevent others taking their place. If you miss one or two, when they do

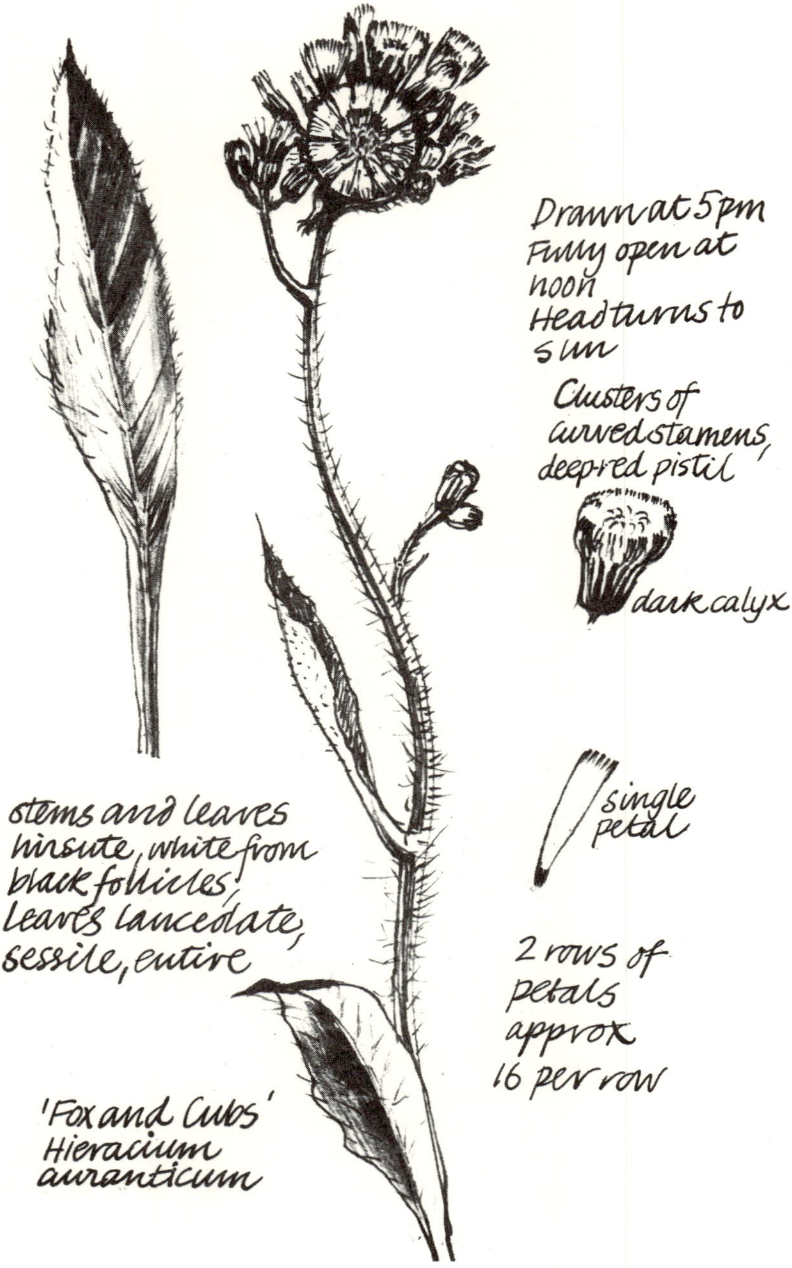

Drawn at 5 pm
Fully open at
noon
Head turns to
sun

Clusters of
curved stamens,
deep-red pistil

dark calyx

single
petal

2 rows of
petals
approx
16 per row

stems and leaves
hirsute, white from
black follicles;
leaves lancedate,
sessile, entire

'Fox and Cubs'
Hieracium
auranticum

appear it is easier to pull them out of the opened-up soil, and certainly you will be compelled to get rid of them, as they spoil that lovely dark mass of earth which sets off any plant to perfection.

There are several kinds of peat. Formed of layers of decomposing marsh plants, twigs, leaves, branches and whole trees, droppings of sheep, cattle and birds—in fact, all natural waste materials—it is found to be in layers of differing qualities. The top layer is acid sphagnum peat; the middle layer less acid, and fibrous; and the deep peat even less acid—sometimes even alkaline, depending on the district. Fine-grade sedge peat is best for lawn dressing, sphagnum peat for azaleas, rhododendrons and some heathers which are intolerant of lime.

Peat holds little plant food, and is usually obtainable in fine, medium and coarse grades, each for a purpose. They vary in water-holding properties because of their substance. Sphagnum peat holds most moisture and is used for mulching. Deep peat is compact and more decomposed than the higher layers. It is moist but has little room for air unless mixed with sharp sand. I have used it in error on heathers like *E. cinerea* 'Golden Drop' and 'Rozanne Waterer', both calcifuge, with disastrous results. I rely now on sedge peat, the middle layer, but it must be kept wet at all times. Used as a mulch on a planting of conifers and heathers, one dry summer it baked hard between weekend visits. Had it not been that moisture drains off the lawn at the top of the bank where they are, the plants would have suffered badly. Those that had their roots down to 'water level' were unharmed but two new specimens had to be kept thoroughly watered once it was noticed that they were flagging.

While this drying out is a disadvantage in that it keeps rainfall from soaking into the surface once it is really baked, it is countered by the fact that nutrients are better retained and not leached away into the subsoil so quickly. Obviously a happy medium of moisture is the ideal.

Peat is most useful—in fact, indispensable—where heathers,

azaleas and rhododendrons are planted. The building up of a peat bed has been ably and often described in other, more specialist publications. I shall record here only the fact that I got 'hooked' on heathers as a ground cover without thinking that, desirable though this is said to be, it does not happen instantly. It takes some time for the plants to grow together to smother the ubiquitous weeds, as planting has to allow for ultimate spread. Some eager gardeners like myself will not allow time for this merging and so plant more and more until one day one is forced to own that there are far too many per square foot for the health and well-being of any of the plants. The fact is that you have to put up with hand-weeding for a year or two—and it's no good leaving a single weed, especially of the seeding kind like groundsel, shepherd's purse, speedwell, chickweed, cow parsley and grass.

Mulches added after thorough weeding, just as the peat already mentioned, will help to keep down weeds. Hop manure provides food as well as a mulch; spent hops may be used but have practically no food value; mushroom compost consisting of horse manure and chalk—not good for calcifuge plants—may sometimes have gypsum instead of chalk, and so could be used without discrimination because it is neutral. If in any doubt, don't use for your favourite rhododendron.

Sawdust must be well weathered before use and then is of doubtful value as moisture is retained and this may rot the plant stems. In my garden, as soon as this light kind of mulch dries out in the sun and wind, it gets whipped away round the stems of plants in a sheltered corner, where it builds up like a snowdrift. Rain falls, and the plants finally succumb.

Lawnmowings have the same drawback, and to add to that, in my garden no mowings are likely to be weed-free. After one attempt when the weeds grew thick and fast through some blackcurrant bushes which I had mulched, the idea was abandoned. It had taken a great deal of time and patience to weed a wide area round those bushes before mulching, too! People who do use lawnmowings warn against those from the first cut after treatment for weeds, as well as the weed-and-feed type of application. There is always the danger of a residue of weedkiller remaining in the cuttings effectively killing off the plants being mulched.

After five years' planting, ground cover is as good a mulch as any, keeping down weeds and providing nutriment in leaf fall, as well as coolness for the roots of plants demanding this as part of their growing conditions. Even evergreens shed old leaves, but new ones grow quickly to replace them so we scarcely notice any change. Grass is ground cover itself, the most inexpensive except in terms of mower power, but it is best in quantity and where planned, and not in isolated tufts among the roses. It is an interesting thought, as you pull away at some of the weeds mentioned above, that some of them are actually cultivated: veronicas are a higher species of speedwell, that pretty little blue flower which spreads so iniquitously that it smothers choicer plants. And

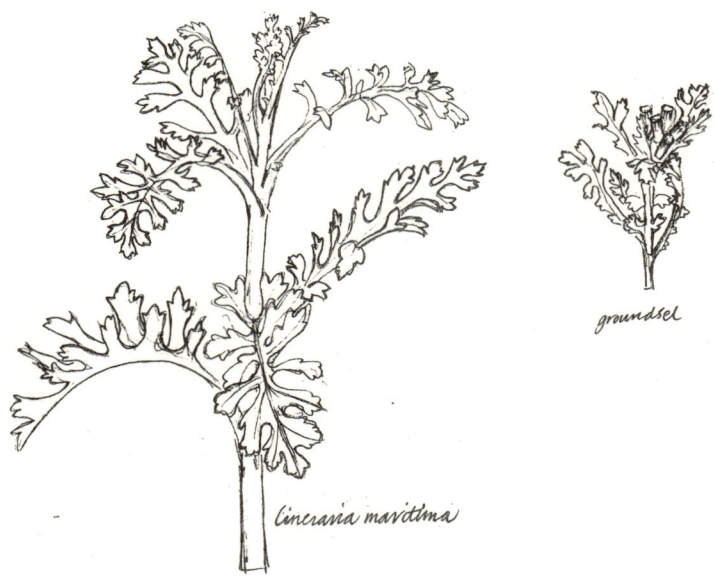

groundsel

Cineraria maritima

the grey-leaved *Cineraria maritima* is really a groundsel in disguise, just as angelica and giant hemlock are nothing but another kind of cow parsley. Artemisias are closely related to yarrow, echinops to thistles, and so on.

Almost any book on gardening will go into raptures about weeding in the herb garden. Just reading about it is one thing; to do it is an experience worth having. Out of curiosity more than anything—except, perhaps, the need to cover the bare earth quickly and cheaply—I bought a packet of fennel, hyssop, sage, balm, chives, and half a dozen roots of thyme. On planting out these roots I found that they were easy to divide and so they were set out, poor little wispy things, all round the edge of one bed. They have since flowered profusely in their first year and have grown into a thick 6in high hedge which gets a light trim after flowering time to keep it bulky. The various scents that arise as one brushes against the leaves of the herbs are more exotic than Chanel No 5 or my favourite Vent Vert.

Weeding aubrieta and other edging, ground-hugging plants which overgrow grass edges so that there is more grass than plants, can be achieved by gently laying back the mass of the plant on to the bed, allowing the grass to slip through until you can see its roots. Grab them and ease them out of the soil, gently disentangling from the plant. Very often pieces of the plant come away with the weeds. If you have sufficient patience, these can be cleaned of weeds and stuffed into the soil in bunches, where they root again quite quickly.

When you have achieved the weed-suppressing carpet of ground cover, with perhaps only the odd one needing extraction from time to time, this is a splendid opportunity to sit back and slack off a bit, to admire one's acquisitions and perhaps to revive pleasant memories of donors, occasions or places from whence they came. Unless you have a garden the size of a young park, watch out for *Lamium galeobdolon.* A sort of dead-nettle, it is a rampant grower and certainly will cover the ground quickly and

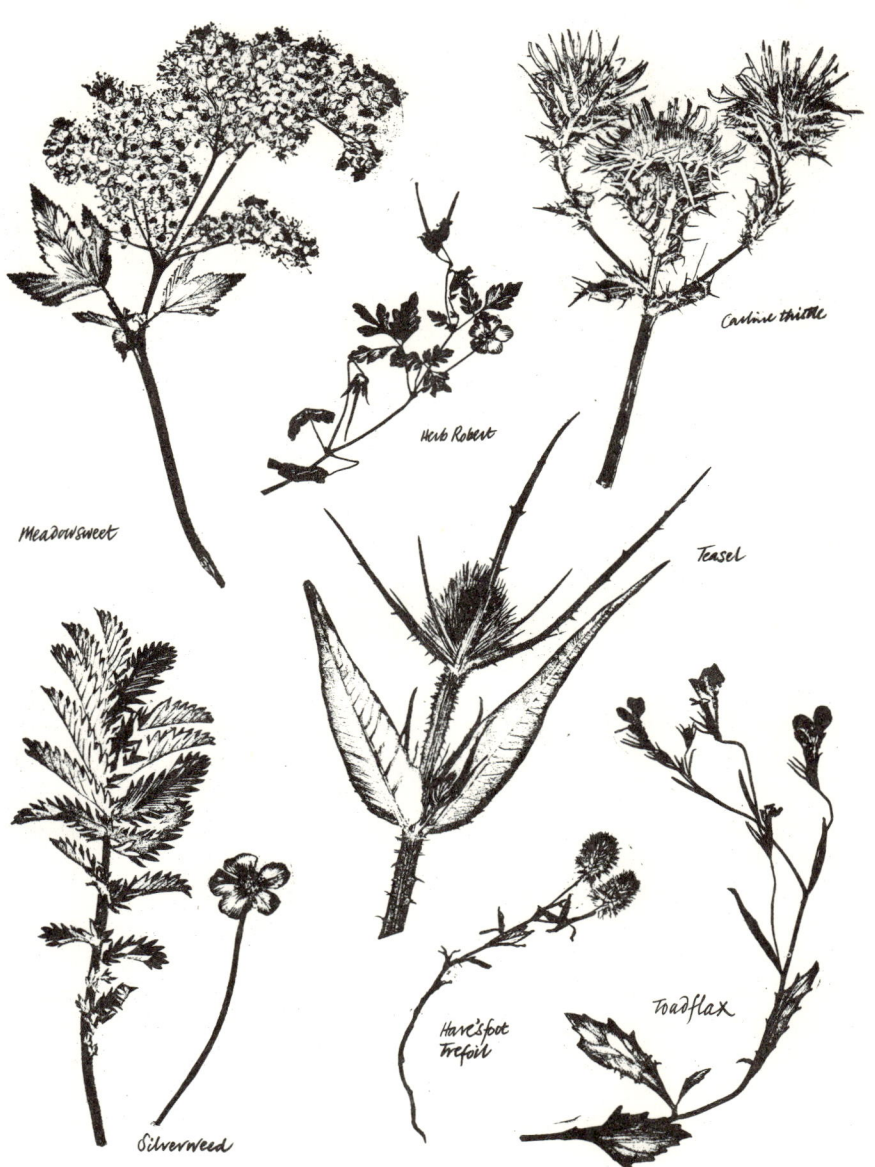

Meadowsweet

Herb Robert

Carline thistle

Teasel

Silverweed

Hare's foot
Trefoil

Toadflax

thickly but at some cost to other plants under whose feet you put it. Growing happily in shade, the variegated sort will enliven dark patches of shadow with its white-striped leaves, but it is difficult to eradicate if you decide to move it elsewhere.

This reminds me of the horrors of bindweed and ground elder, both weeds which waste so much valuable time if allowed to establish. Several 'cures' have been suggested: with bindweed, one is to gather up the several shoots which it puts out from one root and stuff their heads into a jamjar with some paraquat at the bottom. If all the tips can be got into the liquid, it is absorbed and taken down to the roots. But this means leaving a poisonous liquid at large, and one rarely gets all the weed at once, so I prefer to use the more tiresome but thorough method of hand-weeding, digging carefully and deeply enough to avoid breaking a single piece of the root system. If any root is left behind, another lot of the bindweed starts its lusty way up the leg of the nearest plant like a cobra, squeezing it to death.

On ground elder, having tried smothering it with grasscuttings and growing clumps of common marigold among it (said by some to be certain cures), I can only make an impression by first watering with SBK (standing for Synchemicals Brushwood Killer) and then, a day or two later, using the flame gun on the patch of ground elder. In this way about a foot-wide strip of ground has been cleared into the wood at the top of the garden, whence come all these 'nasties'.

Weeds grow more thickly and quickly in ground that is turned over frequently, for example where vegetables are planted and the hoe is used. The latest preventatives, like simazine, work on the principle that the ground should be thoroughly weeded first and then covered with the product and left undisturbed. This would be fine, but in my garden it is impossible, as moles emerge from beneath the earth, to join rabbits, birds and rats, to say nothing of the cats always rooting about, disturbing the soil, undoing all the good work. Even so, there is no doubt that the

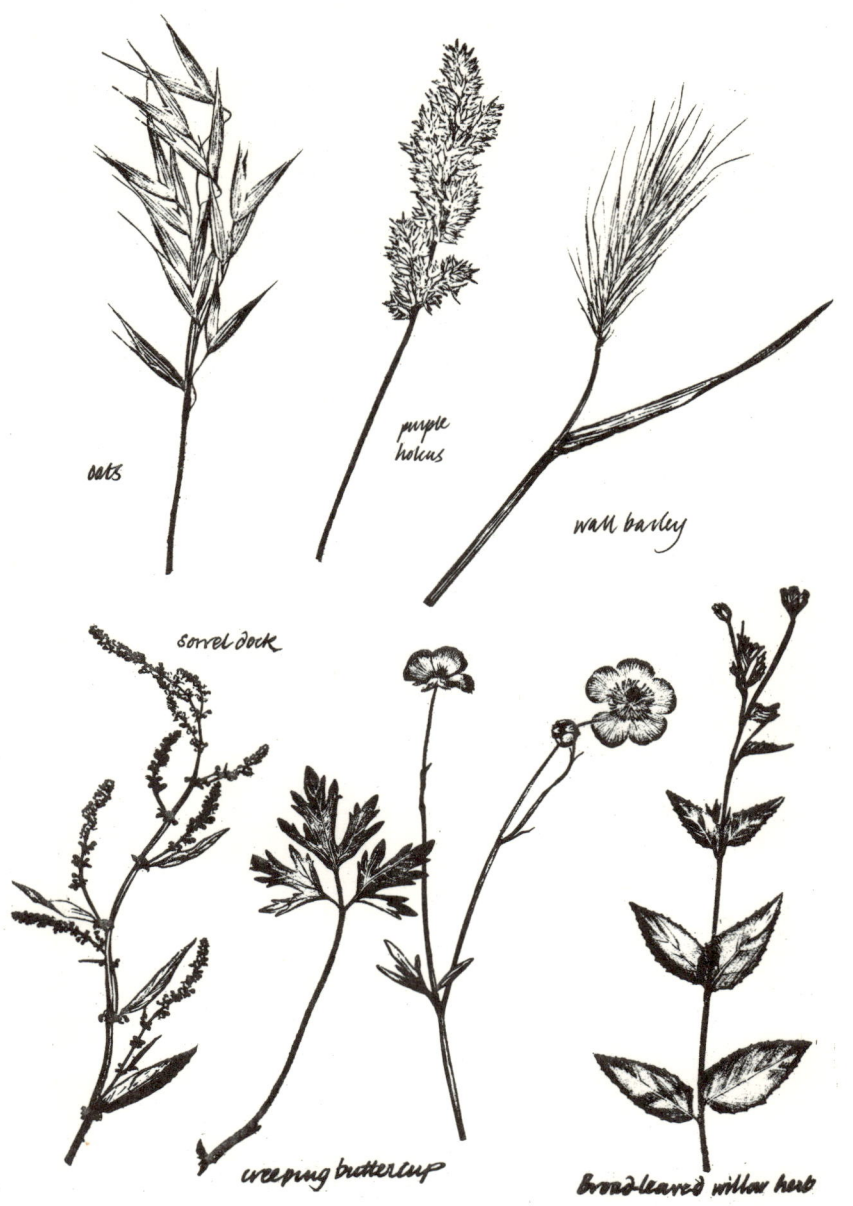

oats

purple
hokus

wall barley

sorrel dock

creeping buttercup

Broad-leaved willow herb

thick new crop of nettles which instantly grew up to take the place of those so painstakingly removed from a potential shrubbery would have been more widespread without the simazine. Only a few very wilting nettles and other weeds grew up over the area that had been treated with simazine. These were uprooted and the area covered again with the product.

Even gardens in towns will suffer from the soil disturbance of birds taking dust-baths, and of dogs and cats. After spending the whole of one Sunday morning weeding the rose garden at my parents' home, and covering the beautiful clean-looking soil with simazine, almost as I turned away, two big blackbirds came winging down to investigate this phenomenon. A brief fight for the privilege of having first peck, and there was my morning's work all over the surrounding paving. Having rid the place of their unwelcome presence, the next visitor was the ginger tom from next door. I gave up.

There is no quick, tireless, absolutely certain and easy method of ridding a garden of weeds except to get right down to it and dig them out. After that, I pin my faith on that nice black peat which comes in such pretty orange bags, and mulch with it as I go. It all takes a surprising amount of time, but is well worth the effort.

Chapter 4

Shedwork

A TOOLSHED is needed by every gardener. The big shed which went with the house was just large enough for a small car, but was in a bad state of dilapidation, with one door propped up beside the main structure. The strong winds which rush up the Brett valley, trying to find outlets up the escarpments on either side, most certainly had utilised the gap between the house and the shed, and in doing so had hit the shed full tilt, pushing up under the corrugated-iron roof overhang in front and getting between the gaps in the planks of the doors.

At first the only entrance was at the front. There was a bench along the garden side, and at the back only a 4ft dwarf could have stood erect. The roof was rusting away and one or two sheets of 'tin', as it is known locally, had blown away up the garden. As a temporary measure, these were rescued and nailed back into position, the whole place groaning at each hammer blow.

A great many catalogues were consulted for a new or second-hand garage at a price I could afford. There was nothing. Besides, I rather liked the look of the faded blue paint on the woodwork, and although tumble-down, it had a certain *je ne sais quoi*. Perhaps its appeal was in its elementary construction, roughly of the same standard of carpentry as my own, so that anything I did to it would blend in.

So I decided to reinforce the skeleton, which was almost entirely of tree trunks nailed together and full of woodworm. I would gladly have removed the old wood, but although the whole place seemed to shake if one so much as tapped it with a finger, those main timbers were immovable. An order for 3in × 3in and 4in × 3in timber was placed with the local supplier, and then I suddenly decided to take this opportunity to add a foot or two to the length of the shed, so more tongued and grooved boarding was ordered for that. The extra length would enable the bench to go on the back wall instead of at the side, and I planned to dig out the earth floor at the back end, so that one could work at the bench. The idea was that carpentry still required for the house should be done at that bench, but from the moment that it was installed, the top of it was littered with bits and pieces, and was only cleared as a gesture when my father was coming to stay.

Even after the extra 2ft 6in had been added, it was evident that it would be very difficult to store big things like the new wheelbarrow and a lawn mower, if the shed were used to keep the car in, so I ordered a small cedarwood shed to take the place of the old spider-ridden Elsan shed behind the garage.

The shed was ordered in September. It arrived the following January. In the meantime, there was the old shed to pull down, the base to enlarge and a wooden floor to make, since floors cost extra on the prefabricated system. I set to work to dig deep holes to receive the supporting timbers for the old shed which was to become the garage. A more frustrating task it would be difficult to find. As one dug, the earth, being dried to little more than dust, would refill the hole in no time at all, and the nice clean holes supposed to be filled out with hardcore could only be induced a foot deep. This was no good. So the roof was taken off over the bits where the new framework was being made and those previously creosoted timbers were driven into the ground. They obliged just enough for the calculated roof height, and so were hastily filled round with stones and cemented in. Luckily the weather was good, and relatively windless, or there might have been some terrible bangings in the night from the loose corrugated iron.

The cross beams had been roughly jointed (my carpentry leaves much to be desired) and screws half driven in, ready to be driven home once they had been aligned with holes drilled in the upright posts. Nothing was being left to chance. My father laughed when he saw the enormous timber frame and the huge screws I'd used, but he was forced to agree that circumstances alter cases, and a neat little garden shed in a suburban area was rather different from a big shed on a windy hillside. The cross beams were further strengthened by what I was pleased to call tie beams; actually, short supporting pieces from the upright to the cross beam, on the gibbet principle. There was only one snag, apart from the hard labour involved, and this was that in driving one of the uprights home into the soil, I must have leaned rather heavily on the hammer, and the post went in some two inches further than it should have. This meant that the shed would lean towards my neighbour's at that corner. I was touchy about making a good job of it, so tried to get the post out again, to fill under and raise it to the correct height. But it must have met some hardcore lower down and jammed between two rocky pieces, and was impossible to move. There was nothing for it but to press on and see what happened.

It was quite difficult to make windows to fit the end where the bench was to be, as this was, as a frame, now wildly out of square. However, when it came to putting the roof on, this was actually a happy accident, as the shed wall nearest the garden (and opposite to the out-of-true upright) had a lean in the right direction which I had tried at the outset to correct, but had proved beyond my strength. The two faults tied nicely together —or at least, that's my story and I'm sticking to it.

The most difficult thing with both these old sheds was to pull them to pieces; it looked very easy as they both seemed so wobbly.

One of the best birthday gifts I ever had was a crowbar, presented with a piece of blue satin ribbon round its tummy. One end was for levering and the other for getting nails out of horses' hoofs, or something. Anyway, it was marvellous for prising up the corrugated iron, however rusty, from the worm-eaten timbers. They clung together like lovers.

a girls best friend

Conversely, it was really satisfying, having demolished enough of the roof to get a series of new pieces of corrugated iron in place, to feel the roof nails being driven home into new heavy timber, and to feel the slight twist, on the shank of the galvanised nails, bite into the wood and pull the roof towards it, and to know that once there, the rubber collars on each would prevent water getting down on to the wood. Working from the back end of the slope towards the front, it was good to find that my calculated overhang at the front was no more than 6in, so that as little wind resistance as possible was offered. The frame up and the roof on, the next nice game to play was to make the windows in the extension and glaze them. Not being sure that I could make them really weatherproof if they were puttied in, and because I had some sliding door channel left over from the bedroom cupboards, I decided to make the windows slide. This also made it possible to disguise the fact that I can't cut glass for anything. The glass slides past the upright in the centre of the window frame and its out-of-square shape shows only when the windows are open and

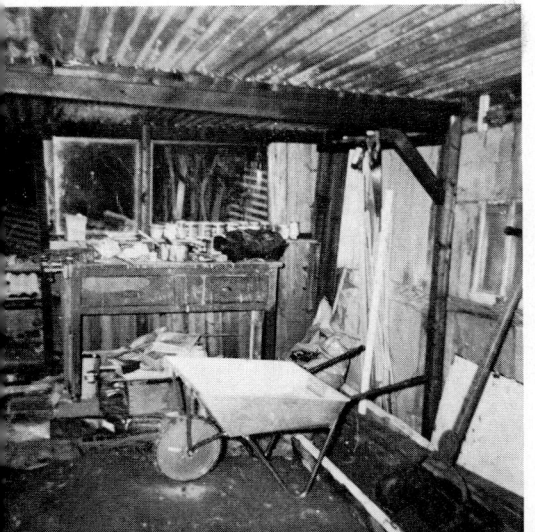

Page 49 (above) The dilapidated house and overgrown garden; (below left) The rehabilitated 'garage', with the bench at the far end, the roof supported on gibbets and the floor dug into the hillside, so enabling tall people to work at the bench; (below right) Heather and rhododendron bed in front of the well. Holly trees in the distance are on the far side of the next-door garden

Page 50 A display of tools to whet any gardener's appetite. This is where dreams of a ride-on mower begin

away from this post. Yes, I *know* it sets a bad example even to mention this cobbling job, but since it had started out that way, there seemed no reason not to continue the tradition.

So that one could stand upright in comfort, earth had to be dug out of the back end of the shed where the bench was to go. This seemed easy at first, but became backbreaking once the dusty crust had been lifted off. The house was built on the side of Barrow Hill, and every time the spade struck something solid, my mind's eye saw Roman treasure—or Victorian at least. But no, it was a very mundane lot of rubbish that came to light. Still, when I was able to stand upright at the window opening, it was a triumphant moment, and, although I was exhausted, I simply *had* to move the bench across and prop it in position. Next day, it was set level and anchored in bricks. The door from the old loo, very solid and surprisingly without worm, was taken off and remounted to the back of the shed, and a bent nail put in to serve as a door catch—it still does. The job was done.

Now for the demolition of the loo. Its state has already been mentioned. It really gave the impression that a puff of wind would blow it over, and that the only reason it had not succumbed before was that the gales blew from a direction which left the little shed in the lee of the big one. After the experience of trying to prise the roof off the big shed it was not really surprising, only displeasing, to find out just how tough it was.

The bloke who put that together used 6in nails in 3in timber and what came out the other side, he just bent over with another swipe of his hammer. I can just see him doing it. If when we die, we are allowed to have a look at what's happening on earth from time to time, that man would have been laughing himself silly, sitting up there smugly on his little cloud watching some fool trying to undo his handiwork. It was hacked at and bashed at until little by little all those dreadful spiders' haunts were laid bare. Gardening gloves prevented splinters and rusty nails from damaging my hands, but by far the best job they did was to keep me out of contact with the spiders' webs. A wonderful bonfire was made and all the old bits of lino which were supposed to keep the draughts from one's bare bottom were thrown on to it, along with the cocoons, webs, creeper and dirt. Another victory.

Making the base for the new small shed tried my uncertain carpentry to its utmost but at last the job was done—and the base immovable. It had been made up and creosoted on the floor of the big shed where all the timber was stored, as I had thought it would not be too difficult nor too big to take out of the front door and round to the concrete base which had been enlarged to fit the new shed size. But it was too heavy.

Luckily a cement lorry had just broken down on the corner of the lane, when I had made this profound discovery, and the driver and his mate came up to the house to ask to use the telephone. While the driver was speaking, his mate was standing about looking a bit lost, so on the basis of labour as payment for the phone call, instead of money which had been offered, I explained what had happened and asked the mate to help me. He was a bit taken aback (thinking of his union rules?) but suddenly seeing the joke, he roared with laughter and willingly lent a hand to get this great wooden raft designed as an anchor against the wind, into place. And none too soon, for the next day the shed was delivered. It was so fragile by comparison with the base that I was aghast. £25 for that bit of rubbish? Still, it was only four walls and a roof to deal with, not sheet after sheet of heavy corrugated iron.

For some reason which now escapes me—perhaps the construction clues were too difficult to follow—I telephoned to John at Snape, and he offered to come over and help me put the shed up. This was a handsome gesture, as he was busy making structural alterations to his own house. Still, an architect ought to know by instinct which bit went where. John came, and I at least spent a lazy day in the January sunshine, supporting the walls of the shed, handing tools when requested and sometimes being allowed to supply those which John had forgotten to bring. One of the greatest comforts arising out of this episode was to hear later through a mutual friend that John thought highly of my ability to distinguish between a wheelbrace and a hand-drill, and was able to anticipate his need for a particular tool.

The other good thing was that from the roof of the old loo shed thirty perfect pantiles were rescued, for which I have yet to find some deserving structure; but I am in no hurry for there is that sort of peace in the atmosphere which makes one regulate one's city patter to the slower stride of the countryman on his feet from dawn till dusk and therefore an instinctive master in the art of energy conservation.

Chapter 5

More Helping Hands

EVENTUALLY the day came when it was possible to repay some of my friends' kindnesses by offering them a weekend in the country. Without exception, they all loved the little house. My parents were invited, having previously heard no whisper of the project. Astonishment amounting to incredulity was expressed.

With eighty-year-olds one is not very sanguine about their ability to climb steep stairs, even though there were fewer of these than at home. But they both managed easily after a bit of practice, though Father's size twelves were a problem on $7\frac{1}{2}$ in treads worn away by woodworm to a cliff-hanging 6in. He soon developed my crab approach and fortunately the décor was approved, the beds declared comfortable and the lack of jet aircraft a distinct improvement to living on the fringes of London Airport.

Naomi and Bryan, the inaugurators of the whole venture, came for a short time and were gratifyingly congratulatory about the changes which had taken place since they first saw the property. An old stone washing copper had been demolished to make room for the larder, and much reconditioning of rotten wood had been done. Bryan's parting shot was 'Now you'll have to do something about the garden.' It certainly was a shambles, even though the newly discovered paved area was admired. There was a great

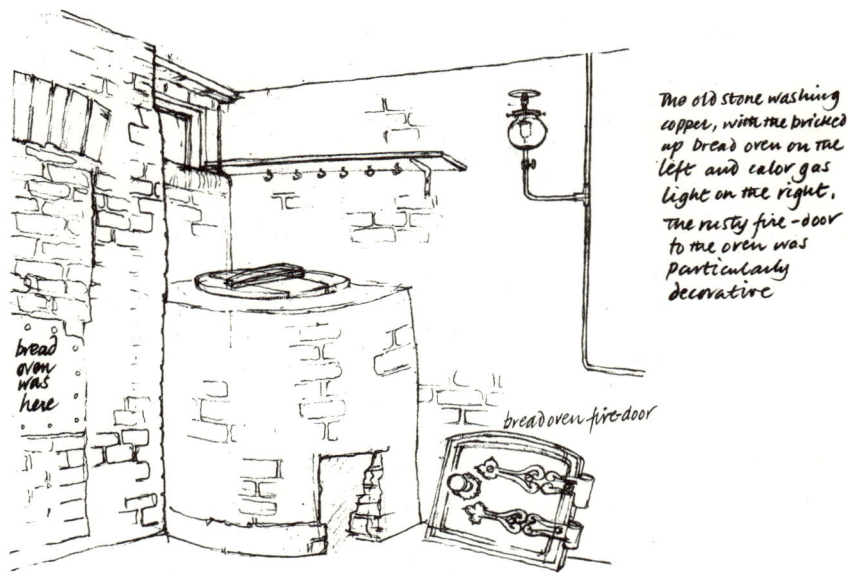

The old stone washing copper, with the bricked up bread oven on the left and calor gas light on the right.
The rusty fire-door to the oven was particularly decorative

bread oven was here

bread oven fire-door

deal still to do, even to make the view from the back door look reasonably organised and weed-free.

Then Kay and Christopher came twice within quite a short time. Chris was a great help with the pathmaking. The tracks, well trodden by the builders on either side of their trench and manholes, have already been mentioned. These tracks I proposed to adopt as permanent but as they were very muddy in winter, they were to be concreted and so needed some hardcore.

'Easy,' Chris said. 'Just look at the garden—full of stones. You and Kay collect the stones and I'll ram them down for you.'

Obediently we got boxes in which to gather the stones, and he found the rammer, and we set to work. Soon Kay and I were streaked with dirt and sweat and our fingernails were broken. There was Chris, imperturbably ramming away like mad and making encouraging noises when he had run out of stones to ram.

A paved or cemented path was an obvious necessity. Never

having done any cementing before, I chose to set out at intervals pre-cast concrete paving slabs in three colours which appeared to accord best with earth and plants: pale and dark grey, and ochre. These were to be cemented in and my collection of beach stones inserted between the paving stones as decoration. As well as the fiddling business of making sure that each beach stone had enough cement round it and slightly on top of it, to keep it in position when the path was used, a lot was learned from making the path.

First, it should have been twice as wide as the 2ft allowed, because the edging plants fill out and overhang, and the taller ones drip icy rain drops down one's neck after a shower, so that one gets wet at both ends. Next, consideration should be given to a path needed for other things apart from just walking from one part of the garden to another. Mowers and wheelbarrows full of prunings and other tricky loads have to be accommodated, and life is much easier if a path is flat—not with lumps of pre-cast concrete and beach stones in it—and without tight corners, since mowers rarely have the wheel lock of a London taxi. The other essential is to make the path on a firm base to avoid sinkage.

Chris had done nobly with the rammer, but that was at least a year before concreting was started, and sand would be needed to bed down the paving stones. This was found in a heap of what looked like earth, at the back of the well, but turned out to be a pile of stones covered generously with sandy gravel. What could be better? Except for the fact that I was too impatient to get the work done and so skimped this job of bedding down, the paths have all been very successful, and have allowed work to continue all through the winter months.

Building the paths was a great trial of strength as well as patience. Certainly I had not realised how tiring mixing cement can be. Of course I should have hired a machine, or a man, but time again was an important factor so the task went steadily on until there were no more paving stones, and more cement was needed. As the next path was a subsidiary, Marleymix was used and the beach stones omitted, in the pious hope that this would save time and labour. Not a bit of it.

When the mix is carted from one place to another in its polythene sacks, the larger aggregate gets up to the top and the cement proper is found at the bottom of the bag. So, when it is turned out on to the mixing base, it still has to be dry-mixed, and then that dragging wet-mix has to be done too. The other drawback is that it is not easy for the amateur to get a good finish. I found that the cement trowel was always catching on the aggregate. But the little path was finished, and for a whim it was signed and dated in the wet cement 'DOUGHERTY 1970'. After all, it was a work of art—it certainly was not a craftsman's job.

On the second visit, Chris showed me how to use the Sheen flame gun, simply by reading the instructions prudently printed on the thing by the manufacturer, and by not being such a coward. True, I could read, but had visions of not being able to control the forest fire I *knew* would be started with the Terrible Torch, and had to wait until someone set a good example before I could bring myself to try. Once used, it was found to be an easy and invaluable aid for keeping weeds in check, but it does make rather an alarming roar when it really gets going. This brought the neighbours out to strategic points in their gardens to see what this mad woman from London thought she was up to now. It is no substitute for digging and weeding properly— something which I learned in time about its potential as a time and labour saver. The intense heat concentrated on a small area at the end of the flame kills weed seeds and growth of the moment, but the flame gun should be used regularly to keep the weeds really in check. Once a week might be enough, but if several weeks are missed because there are more urgent things to do, the weeds grow up again. There is no denying that it is a valuable item in any tool shed, though.

All my friends who visited the house (and some who have not yet been) contributed something: work, plants, ideas, information. I treasure the memory of Pat solemnly cutting the long grass round a mullein which arose out of the 'rough'. Along I came, seconds later, with the mower and chopped it down, not knowing then what it was nor that she had specially preserved it. She also

alluded to the garden as 'wild' which I thought sounded a bit derogatory, but knowing Pat, thought it impossible that she should say so, if indeed it meant what I thought. In later conversation it appeared that this was a desirable thing and that very well laid out 'set pieces' were not to her taste. Taste or no taste, I had no choice, since I knew so little about plants in those days that quite certainly many a treasure was pulled up or cut down, like the mullein, without my realising its value. Equally, I felt it would be folly to transplant anything which looked like growing, even though it might not be in a particularly pleasing situation.

At first, seed was sown—and very unprofessionally, as I see now in retrospect. Sowing seed is quite the cheapest way of obtaining a lot of plants for a large garden. But finding that few of the seedlings materialised, I concluded that they, too, had been pulled up as the dreaded weeds, without my knowing the difference.

So much depends on what one requires a garden to be. Neat and tidy? Only in suburban or town gardens where there are few free-flying weed seeds the year round, or in a country garden with many hands on the job. Colourful? It can be too much so, as I found after my first summer season. Dahlias, lupins, roses, resident peonies, red-hot pokers, wallflowers, the lot—a riot of colour which was uncontrolled and looked so. Gradually since then I have moved things about, or discarded them, all the time working towards a garden which can be enjoyed instead of always having to be worked away at. That is my kind of garden, and no doubt many others' too.

The first sunflowers were grown that year. They were well over 8ft tall and my neighbour was quite envious, so that when they came to the seed stage, one of the enormous heads like great textured plates of 9–10in diameter was given to him. Some of mine seeded themselves on the compost heap but, even so, were not such splendid specimens as the originals.

Another friend, Dorothy, brought me a hellebore. I had dimly heard of these, and as Dorothy is such a keen and knowledgeable gardener, I knew it must be something special, although she spoke of it so lightly. The hellebore was given a place of honour right outside the back door where it could be seen every time my visitors and I came and went. Only some months later when

Hellebore corsicus

it was well established and growing on, did I read that hellebores like shady places. Despite the fact that I had chosen the hottest, most sunny spot in the garden, it has flourished and carried great buds so early in the year that I despaired of ever seeing them open, because the searing wind came up the side of the hill and through the funnel between the house and the garage spreading out right across the face of the hellebore in bud. The first year I instinctively placed screens around it, and then the frosts came, and snow, and there were still no signs of the buds opening. What a sensible plant—it waited until there was at least a chance of some sun to warm it. Then those incredible green saucer-shaped flowers appeared, with long yellow stamens. The whole plant was covered with them. It was then possible to identify it

← wispy dead stamens →

↑ pale viridian, veined purple inside even more purple outside

← leaves wrapped round stem

← very dark purple-spotted lower down

Hellebore orientalis atrorubens

as *Helleborus corsicus*, and since then I have collected *Helleborus niger*, the Christmas rose, and *Helleborus orientalis atrorubens*, a really exciting and dusky beauty.

My neighbour, Basil, often asks whether I take any time off to enjoy the garden, instead of always having my nose to the ground like a hound on the scent of something good. He's much too polite to put it quite like that, but the message gets through all the same, and I relax for a bit. But there's always something new and exciting to be done or discovered, and it is such a great pleasure to be doing it here.

Chapter 6

Tools and Equipment

EVERY time my parents came to stay it seemed the garden was given some new piece of equipment. There was the wheelbarrow which had to have its wheel removed so that it could travel home in state beside Father in the car. Since then a variety of two-wheeled barrows have become available. Two wheels take all the weight of the load; with one wheel the gardener takes half the weight herself.

Then a lawnmower became essential and was found and the front grass given its first cut six months after the purchase of the house. By this time it was really shaggy. With the edges laboriously clipped too, it all looked very trim—and I resolved to buy some long-handled shears. It is possible to get a fitting for these to catch the cuttings and remove the litter to the wheelbarrow rather than let it lie or gather it by hand later. I didn't have much success with mine, but the principle appeals to me and no doubt I fixed it wrongly. Then there are those battery-powered or mains electric edging devices which are intended to make this chore easier. Before getting one of these—quite apart from the question of being able to afford one—a good deep gutter must be cut all along the lawn's edges to make clean edges on which to work, and the sides of the lawn should be flat in order to allow the wheels of the tool to run smoothly.

The hedges still had to be hand-sheared, and it was two more years before I was able to launch out and buy electric gear. Despite the trailing cable, this is to be highly recommended as it takes hours off a boring job, as well as reducing the hard labour so that one feels free and fresher to deal with other tasks. A cable winder was added to the stock in the toolshed, and some stakes, made of plastics-covered iron with a very convenient open loop at the top, placed at intervals up the garden from the power point, proved useful supports (like telegraph poles) for the cable in action. Now the latest development in this field, obvious after the domestic cordless shaver, is a battery hedge-cutter run off nickel-cadmium batteries rechargeable from the mains: so much easier to use, and lighter too.

The following year some means had to be found for cutting the 'rough', the piece of ground between the cultivated garden and the row of blackcurrant bushes which can be seen on the frontispiece plan. I developed a conscience about this at a very early stage, seeing what a variety of weeds grew among the grass and trees: nettles, of course (though fewer in that area), docks, plantains, thistles, dandelions by the score, and all the smaller fry of seeding weeds that can be called to mind. My neighbour Basil dug his garden next to this patch and planted vegetables in lovely tidy rows. Knowing that he did this after a hard day's work on the family farm, I was not going to make his labour harder by passing on all my weeds to him. Previously the heads had been chopped off with the reap hook, but now I went on strike and called in a local supplier to bring me a Flymo.

Desmond arrived with a demonstration model which he had great difficulty in starting, though he assured me that it had been all right at the shop. *Pace* Flymo! It may be that he had not acquired the knack of pulling that wretched lanyard, or that there was a jinx on that particular machine. The poor sweating chap at last got it started and it went for a short while, then stopped again. I tried pulling on the lanyard, and simply could not get to the end of it to give that vital thrust to start the engine. It must have been designed with an ape in mind. I am very tall, with arms to match, but I could never have started that mower. It was for this reason that I had asked for the demonstration, having been warned of this difficulty; also I wanted to be assured by someone with experience that my choice of mower would be suitable for my ground, which was far from level. Then I found that the Flymo does not have a grass-box—naturally enough since it huffs out grass all round its skirt—and on to the flower beds go all the grass and weed seeds. That, and the lanyard start, decided me against it, though of course the Flymo is ideal for other types of garden, especially for banks. Now there is an electrically powered version.

As I walked down the garden and out to the van with him, Desmond said, 'I don't know whether you would consider a rotary grass-cutter on wheels. It's a bit more expensive but you can get a grass-box for it, and it has a wind-up starter which most ladies find easier. I'm taking this one up to the district nurse, who tried out a friend's and has now ordered one for herself, because she said it was the only one of its kind that she had been able to start the first time.' It was a few pounds more than the Flymo, but when he demonstrated it, I saw immediately that being more suited to my terrain this would have advantages for me and would be worth the extra expenditure.

And so, a few days later, the Mountfield M4 was delivered, together with the right mixture of petrol and oil, and the taming of the 'rough' began. Desmond had said that in a year or two's time the difference made by regular cutting would be amazing, and he was absolutely right. In fact, the difference made by that first mowing, even with the blade set at its highest, was considerable and very heartening. The second year after buying the Mountfield the change in the appearance of the 'rough' is very obvious from numerous photographs taken at every stage in the garden's development. It was Pat, so patiently using the shears on the encroaching grass, who first made me see what a difference it would make if all the grass were cut.

After a good spell of really hard grass-cutting over several years with the two-stroke, the starting gear began to give trouble and following several servicings, finally vibrated itself right off the top of the machine. This was a lesson to me to check at frequent intervals all the nuts and screws on a heavy-duty machine. A garden with a large amount of grass to be dealt with in an effort to save the labour of weeding and tending flower beds is a great liability without a reliable mower. In a moment of panic just before the Mountfield first broke down, I had rushed into a London store and bought one of the cheapest of the electric machines which looked very frail beside the tough out-back-type Mountfield. Still, it has proved its worth, keeping the shorter front grass in good order with the minimum of effort all the summer, and even making a good job in the spring of the first cut in those areas within its reach.

Using it while the Mountfield went in for repair, I thought about the whole question of this sort of essential machinery, and came to the conclusion that it was much more sensible to buy a really good machine at the start, the very best one can afford, because in the long term money is saved on repairs and replacements and one's time and temper are preserved. After a short return to work, during which it was apparent from the difficulty in keeping the engine running that something was wearing out, it came as no surprise when the two-stroke completely broke down and was past repair.

Then I decided to get a four-stroke self-propelling machine because of the amount of uphill work on the land. There are, of course, pros and cons: a four-stroke, with separate compartments for oil and petrol, does not like to be tipped sideways on a steep bank in case the engine overheats and burns out. The air-cushioned Flymo is undoubtedly the best machine for that sort of job provided that it can be kept well under control as it is swung to and fro. One hint on the four-stroke front: before

Page 67 (above left) Looking across the front of the terrace bed which is full of experimental foliage combinations; *(above right)* Pride of my heart, *Euphorbia wulfenii*, 18 months old here and now 4ft high; *(below)* Some plants grown for their foliage effect, others for their texture; *(left)* African marigolds make a striking display and attract innumerable peacock butterflies. By contrast, the deeply cut foliage makes an intricate pattern of light and dark; *(right) Cineraria maritima*'s bright silver is startlingly contrasted with the dull green of the rounded hebe and the spiky leaves of *Helleborus corsicus* beyond

Page 68 (above) The whole of the first garden plan evolved from the two paths trodden by the builders beside the septic-tank drainage trench; *(left)* The boat bed from the house; *(right)* The stern end from the upper garden. An unfinished path and a bed full of up-and-coming marguerites can be seen; *(below)* A sunflower seed head. Some 9in across, the great plate of separate seeds is arranged with mathematical precision

kicking the machine because it won't start, check that the petrol is turned on. Also it is wise not to get waylaid by a tree, leaving the mower to wander off on its own, for you to pursue.

After considering the battery-driven machines available, I decided against buying one because of the weight of the battery added to that of the basic machine. The Webb 'Windsor' is as much as I can move around when not under power, and a battery mower under the same conditions on my slopes would be immovable, though I am far from frail. One needs to remember that it may not always be possible to drive the mower from one part of the garden to another, and that brute strength is sometimes required. New mowing machines are being marketed all the time and the choice widens, especially in the field of electric machines. There comes a time, however, when one has to steer clear of temptation—had I not done so I would have a comfortable seat on a big mower right now.

In the line of smaller equipment, it is worth buying the best you can afford. Stainless steel, though costly, is valuable for its strength and length of service. A swoe—Wilkinson Sword's patent and witty name for a very useful tool—was one of the first weeding devices bought. Since it won an award for design, one expects it to be easy and comfortable to use, as well as shapely and good to look at, and it proves to be a lightweight, adaptable hoe. From a friend I inherited a stainless-steel hand fork and trowel, and these withstood a week left outside in bad weather, without a mark.

Green Shield stamps provided many of the first tools for the garden: a lawn aerator, a hose reel, rake, pair of notched shears, small hand fork, and many other things no doubt, if I were to take a look around to remind myself. Used in a reasonable way and *cleaned after use*, they will remain faithful friends for years.

When it comes to pruning gear, most people have their own views. Knowing little about this job, I avoided the pruning knife because it looks so dangerous. Actually the cut is made on the

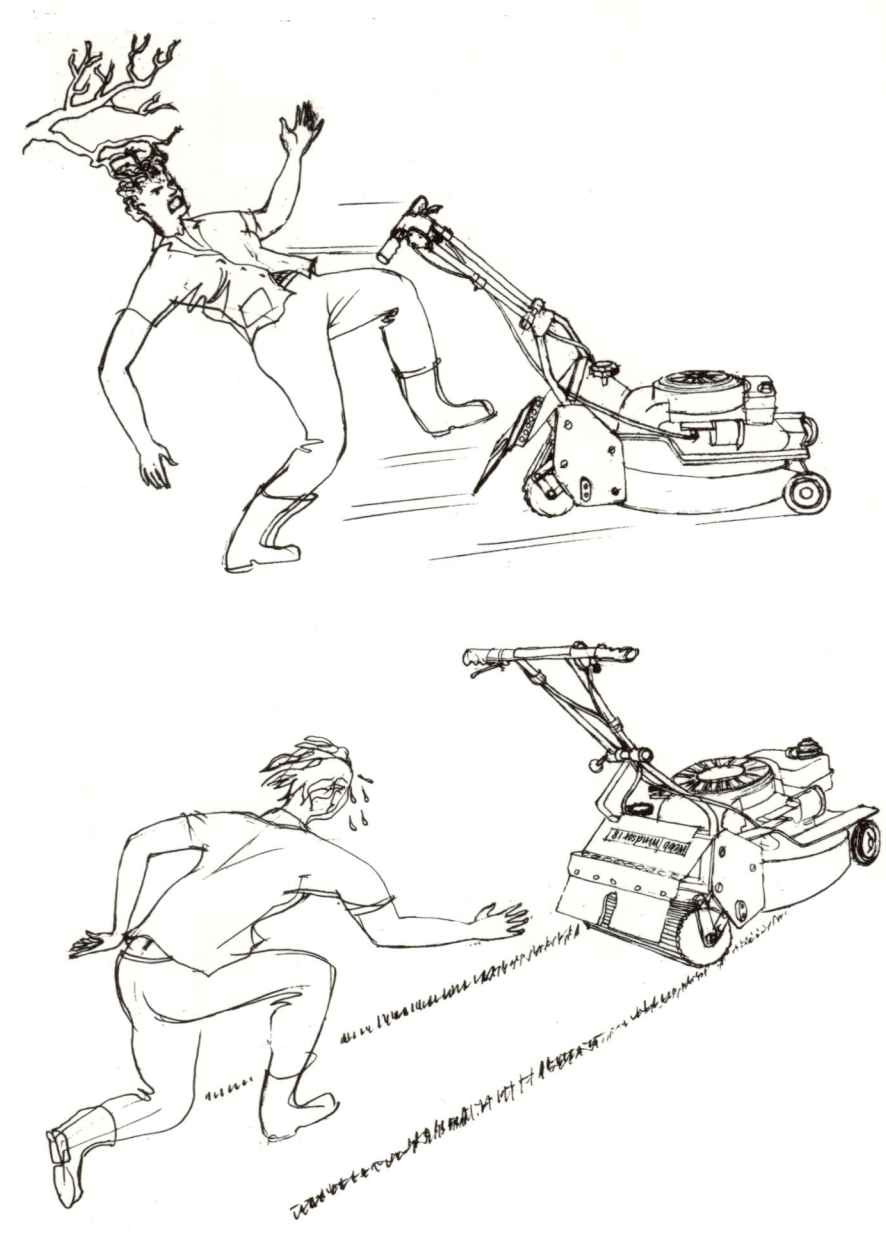

stem of the plant above the point held by the thumb, which does not then act as the anvil and so is saved from harm. Most diagrams of cuts with the pruning knife are not reassuring, so I bought secateurs instead, a small pair for twiggy wood and a heavy-duty pair for the bigger stuff. The rest of the tree pruning is completed with what is variously known as a long-armed pruner, a lopper, or more particularly, 'Little Jupiter', another well-designed tool. The highest branches need a parrot-beaked pruner on a long handle with a pulley action.

There are two kinds of secateurs: anvil and scissor. The latter speaks for itself; the former has one sharpened blade cutting down on to a strip of metal. I have tried both sorts and prefer the anvil type, which seems to have a more positive action and is firmer. Whatever your choice, the tools should be kept very sharp, clean and well oiled. A rub with a clean cloth steeped in Jeyes Fluid ensures that disease is not spread from one plant to another.

A pruning saw is necessary if you have trees to cope with. The saw can be curved, straight and two-edged, but must be made for the purpose—not just any old saw. To keep these tools from rusting, there is a rust-preventative paper, not infallible but better than just letting them lie about in a damp shed. Joints need oiling too, on the saws which fold into a sheath and on the secateurs and pruners.

On one of the few occasions when I allowed myself to be diverted from the weekly trip to Suffolk, Mary and I went down to her cottage near Sidmouth. That weekend she invested in a mower similar to the Mountfield in looks but with a four-stroke engine. At that time I still had the two-stroke, and it was interesting to compare the two machines for performance, details of design and so on. Much more interesting was to prowl round the Sidmouth shops, and to come away with a long-handled, light-weight fork. The length of handle enables one to extract weeds gently from the back of a border without having to put great feet on the bed or the choicest plants. There is also a long-armed weeder, developed for the disabled who cannot bend, but excellent for preventing backache for me too. The same firm makes a long-armed flower-gatherer too, and there is a tool for picking up leaves and hedge trimmings without bending. In fact, if one looks carefully, quite a lot of strain on the back, the gardener's most vulnerable part of the body, can be avoided by having the right equipment.

For those for whom weight-lifting is taboo, the garden roller designed to be filled with water or sand when in use is a convenience. When empty its light weight makes it easy to store. Similarly, instead of using the wire fan-shaped rake for scarifying the lawn, there is a new rake which makes use of its own weight to clean out the dead stuff, avoiding the tiring action of leaning on the traditional wire rake.

Noticing that both my neighbours used spades for digging, I tried it too, but still find it easier to disentangle the weed roots from the soil using a fork, and to pick up the left-overs afterwards by smoothing the surface with the back of the fork and picking up the 'odds' in a bundle like spaghetti. Shortly I hope to be able to treat myself to a Wolf 'Terrex' spade, another useful development for the disabled gardener. It works on the lever principle, enabling one to dig without bending, lifting the earth or shifting the spade. A foot is put on the pedal behind the blade and the pivoting action of the mechanism does the rest. I'm all for easy work, and there are some jobs for which a spade is essential.

Waterbutts are part of the proper equipment of a garden, especially in areas of hard water and low rainfall. All plants benefit from rainwater; the calcifuge ones will tolerate nothing else. Friends laugh when they count the six butts at strategic points around the house and sheds, but the butts can save a great deal of humping of cans of water in summertime and are a great bonus in times of drought. I have even been able to fit a hose to the tap of one butt to water a nearby bed of seedlings. They love their more frequent drinks. A friendly builder suggested that some water be drawn off when the mould-made polystyrene butts were full in winter, in case the water froze, expanded and split the seams of the butts.

In a sense weedkillers are tools of the gardener and so are mentioned here. The blitz on the nettlebed opened my eyes to the possibility of extending their use to other parts of the garden —the brick paths and paving were becoming whiskery and a spot weedkiller was tried out on the broad-leaved weeds on the lawns. This is available in solid wax-like sticks and can just be rubbed into the centre of the weed; alternatively a liquid weedkiller can be painted on.

Weedol is probably the best known of general weedkillers. It acts on the green tissues of plants—any plants, so be careful to keep it off your best beloved. It now contains diquat as well as paraquat and the two together deal with thin and broad-leaved weeds, providing a total coverage of annual and perennial weeds. As these grow inextricably mixed, it is usually necessary to make more than one application. The annuals die off quickly right down to their roots, but the perennials are tougher underground. Leave the weeds to die off and rot into the ground. If you start taking the tops off as soon as you think they are dead, it is more likely to encourage further growth from still-living roots. The younger they are when treated, the less unsightly their dead bodies will look. Weedol can be used round the base of mature trees if you are, as I am, too lazy to cut off the fuzz which the mower won't reach; it will also kill off young suckers.

Weedol does not affect the soil, in fact it is wasted there, but it is as well to wait about three days before planting up an area after extensive application. A special sprinkle-bar applicator is sold in two sizes, one for detailed work round plants and the other for more general application to larger areas. A special polythene container with an extendable spout is also available, but if you use an ordinary watering-can, keep one specially for weedkillers and never use it for watering plants you wish to remain unharmed. It is sensible to label the weedkilling can *permanently*. The usual precautions about use are on the packaging of the product and should be well heeded.

More persistent growth needs tougher treatment, and there is a special product for paths and driveways, for nettles, docks, ground elder, brush wood and so on. An extremely useful leaflet is issued by **WRO** (Weed Research Organisation) giving details of the use, content and effectiveness of the three main types of weedkiller: foliage-applied, like Weedol; foliage-applied, trans-located herbicides like Pathclear and SBK; and soil-applied residual herbicides like Ramrod (simazine) and sodium chlorate.

From personal experience, I find Ramrod excellent after weeding a patch of ground, would never use sodium chlorate unless in danger of being overcome with weeds 10ft tall, and find that a combination of Weedol and the use of the Sheen flame wand (referred to earlier in connection with the nettle war) are very adequate to control an uncomfortably lusty weed-growth each year. It should be remembered that the soil-contact herbi-cides continue to kill off newly germinating weed seeds, so that plants can scarcely be expected to survive if put in after treatment of the soil surface. The treatment is usually effective for at least six months.

Chapter 7

_____

Groundwork

IT is of ever-absorbing fascination to see a plant emerge from what appears to be nothing very substantial, put on leaves, flower gloriously and then, perhaps, as a final gesture, give splendid leaf colour, berries or a beautiful seedpod before it dies. And if a perennial, how much more thought-provoking that the cycle begins all over again next year, and that each plant has its allotted lifetime. As I dig round the garden the difference in scale of every part of the natural world is a thing to be marvelled at and greatly respected; so is the analogous development, but over quite different time spans, of people, plants, insects, trees, even seasons of the year and times of day.

Before deciding what to plant it is worth finding out as much as possible about the life and growth potential of various plants, and in particular of trees, which one may be thinking of planting. This way serious mistakes can be avoided.

How do plants grow? In a word, photosynthesis. That is the reaction of light on the cells composing the foliage, causing chemical changes in the plant. The roots take in water and trace elements from the soil and a chemical chain reaction is set up which releases these nutrients for the plant's use. They thrive on starch and protein and to produce these need, in varying proportions, nitrogen, phosphates and potash; also calcium, magnesium, zinc, iron, sulphur, manganese, copper, boron and molybdenum. The last group are the trace elements already referred to. The others are the essential elements and will only be present in soil 'in good heart', that is which has not been left untreated for many years but has been fed. In nature, leaf fall takes care of a good deal of this feeding, as well as animal manure and birdlime.

Plants 'breathe' through the minute pores on the underside of their leaves. In the daytime they absorb carbon dioxide and give out oxygen. At night this is reversed; thus the old recommendation not to leave plants in the room of a sick person at night. This also explains why so many lovely subjects will not survive on office windowsills, or in areas of high air pollution. The pores become clogged with solids and the plant is literally asphyxiated. Office plants should frequently be sprayed to keep the foliage clean and to counteract the drying effect of central heating or just hot rooms.

To exist at all, plants need a food supply which they get from the earth. A well-balanced mixture of sand, clay, chalk and humus in varying proportions gives a healthy loam or a crumbly soil with tiny air spaces which allow roots to wriggle through and grow, moisture absorption and drainage of any superfluous water. Too much sand allows too swift drainage resulting in a poor foothold for plants, so staking and protection is needed. In clay soil the particles are too closely knit to allow roots to travel and it holds too much moisture.

In sandy soil like mine, it is necessary to make the most of natural drainage. So moisture-loving plants go at the bottom of the slope and sun-lovers and non-sog plants at the top. Seedlings with some protection against a deluge of rain, can be planted at the foot of the slope. The garden is high enough on the whole hillside to have adequate drainage during heavy rain, though since the sandy soil is not retentive, peat has been added on every possible occasion. Where the soil is little more than dust, rain runs away down hill, doing little good. This has to be remedied.

In summer there is some advantage in a slope that runs both sideways and forwards—north to south and east to west—as the garden receives both the excess moisture from the wood of oaks at the top and the drainings from my neighbour's generous use of real animal manure.

Soil from various parts of the garden was tested and found to be slightly acid, more so at the top near the wood and less so lower down, but not neutral or alkaline, thank heavens. In fact, just right for the sort of plants I want to grow. Still, it was a mistake to make a heather bed on top of the clay subsoil left by the builders' trenching. By heather-craze time, however, masses of peat had gone into the ground and once the heathers were planted, sequestrene was regularly applied, and they have survived.

Humus and fertilisers are needed by hungry soil, one to supply bulk and bacteria to improve the texture, the other to release foods already in the soil. Watering and mulching are equally essential, the mulch to be either of bulky organic material (compost, if rotted to a really crumbly state), or well-soaked peat on well-soaked earth. Dry dressing on sandy soil is hopeless as it just blows away. Mulching smothers weeds and keeps plants moist and cool at the roots in summer.

Seaweed manure is very valuable. It is weed-free and should be dug in while wet. It may also be composted in heaps by itself, and is very rich in nitrogen, phosphates and potash. Flies love it too.

Balance of the soil can be improved with fertilisers. The value of lime lies in that it breaks up heavy clay and encourages the presence of bacteria and earthworms, both good for the quality of the soil. Slow-acting fertilisers like bonemeal are best applied to plants during periods of dormancy.

Stony or sandy soil should only be dug lightly, so keeping the food near the surface and available for plants through their fibrous roots. Shallow digging also avoids bringing the infertile subsoil to the surface. As sandy loam slides round the roots of plants very quickly if dry, stake any plant which may need it as you put it into the earth. In this way you can see where the stake should go to avoid root damage.

Stones help to retain moisture. After heavy rainfall the surface of the ground is often littered with smallish stones from which the fine particles of soil have been washed away, rather like the pebbles on the beach when the sea has carried back the sand with the receding waves. If you plunge your hand down under the surface pebbles on a hot day, the stones at the lower level will still be quite damp. Moisture remains under garden stones too. I have made a practice of packing stones round my more precious specimens after mulching well with peat, but not too close to the stems, as it is the tips of the root system which take in moisture. Stony soil is free-draining and can be worked in all but hard frost and snow conditions, though there was one memorable Christmas when I was able to dig up a large patch near the wood when the snow was thick on the rest of the ground.

Soot is said to be beneficial but must be well matured. It can be slung in a sack suspended on a pole in a tub of water, and the water used for feeding. Percy Thrower says that fresh soot is a pesticide, though I have not yet dared to try it out. It is said to drive out slugs and snails, but one is warned not to let it get on to plants, as it scorches their leaves and roots in its fresh state. Left outside for two or three months it is a valuable source of nitrogen, improving the size and colour of leaves, especially of brassicas. Soot should just be dusted on and then hoed or forked in lightly at any time of the year. I liked a recipe for potting cyclamen which I found among my cuttings, which read like one of my mother's cooking recipes: a cupful . . . a pinch . . .

2 parts loam
1 part leaf mould or moss peat
Liberal sprinkling of sand and powdered mortar rubble
Dusting of bonemeal and old soot

By the time that the haphazard start to make a garden out of a wilderness had begun to show results, a year's work had provided some experience of the conditions up and down my particular patch. Others with plans in mind for a new garden might be able to benefit from this. Before deciding on a planting plan, think a bit about climatic conditions—in general, and in particular. I can only speak about the East Anglian, riverside windy patch not far from the estuaries of the rivers Stour and Orwell. There I found that on the slope of that hillside, the lower parts of the garden could easily have become frost traps, except for the opening which lets all the wind through between the house and the garage—so it does have its uses after all. Think also about the amount of sun that different parts of the garden will receive, and the effect on plants nearby of any hedges or trees already *in situ*. Sun-demanding subjects will suffer particularly, growing spindly and weak in an effort to get all the heat and light they need, if put into a shady place by mistake.

Quite the worst aspect of the Suffolk climate is the force of wind, which blows from almost every quarter at different times of the year. This force is most deadly as it sweeps up the side of the house, either downhill from the north-east or uphill from the south-west. It is a wonder that any plants survive at all, but they do, and this is the reason why I have stuck to my rule that if anything succumbs then I shall not try it again. The only exception made is where I know that I have planted something unsuited to harsh treatment right in the line of fire. There are few days when all is still, but the fresh breeze which cools the gardener's brow in summer is very welcome, merely a reminder of the heavier guns to come. The safeguard for plants is proper staking, as we shall see in a later chapter.

Windbreaks are another obvious answer for plant protection: not walling, either pierced and decorative or just plain brick, in my garden, since every element should accord with the 'just-grown-out-of-the-hayfield' aspect. In any case, wind meeting unresisting material creates havoc as it rushes up one side and down the other with increased force, and the pierced walling, which is so popular today, is too modern in character for me. Hedges do well if properly and frequently trimmed to keep them dense; spinneys are better but the trees and shrubs chosen must themselves be very hardy, like quickthorn, ash or some coniferous trees.

Since we are considering basic factors before succumbing to the delights of choosing plants from nurseries or catalogues, a word here about trees will not come amiss. It should be remembered that tall things obscure views and on a windy hillside often become curiously twisted shapes. A plantation of medium-sized subjects is better. The overall texture of the tree-planted area will change, especially over the years as growth increases, and a flat expanse of sky with storm clouds or sunsets, can be replaced by an interlaced pattern of branches. Rooms can be darkened by too large a tree growing too close to the house. It is also worth considering which trees sucker easily, as on my sandy soil if the mower takes a bite into an exposed root, suckers shoot up madly. Alternatively, if rain erodes the soil, roots are exposed and damaged, again causing a rash of suckers. Some trees are particularly prone to this—lilac, sumach and plums to mention only a few.

Catalogues are often misleading. Even though the ultimate size of every plant is stated, it is almost impossible to visualise in 3D terms. Terrible mistakes can be made by innocently planting what appears to be a small shrub or tree, only to find that in ten years' time it is 20ft high and almost as wide, taking all the light and nutriment in the soil away from surrounding plants. Several times I was caught napping over this, though luckily by nothing so permanent as a tree, mostly by packets of annual seeds given me by friends whose gardens were not big enough to accommodate all the free gifts from the gardening magazines they read.

Sweet rocket was the surprise of my life. The first year it made only foliage, but so attractive that the plants were left as they were in an area where ground cover was needed. The following year, true to its name, it rocketed skywards. The flowers smelt very sweetly and looked handsome in their masses of white, pale and dark pinky-mauve, bobbing about in the wind. Butterflies are attracted to them, and I saw quite a few pretty little orange-tips sitting on the flower heads, almost impossible to see when they had folded away their orange markings to reveal only the mottled grey-brown of the underwings.

Balsam was another surprise, from seeds given by my neigh-bour Betty, who did not remember what they were called but said that 'they came up to a good height and had pretty little spikes of hanging flowers'. Either my soil is much more fertile than hers or she had forgotten how tall they grew. She also omitted to warn me that the seed capsules burst when ripe and scatter seed in all directions. The first year I was entranced. The stems and leaves were charmingly red-shot and set off the pink pendulous flowers to perfection. All the plants, set in a colony of about two square yards, were at least five feet high, and some were more, with great succulent stems about an inch in diameter. A great visual success, but the following year there were plants coming up all over the place because I had not uprooted the originals before they seeded. Then I remembered Betty's husband had muttered something about my living to regret the day I was given them, but I thought he was being unduly male-gloomy and took no notice. That second year I made sure all the seedlings were pulled out except where I wanted them.

Honesty is another vigorously seeding plant and unless there is some flower arrangement demanding spikes of grey silken seedpods, one is tempted to leave them on the plant. Not until the outer part of the pod has opened and released the seeds, and it is too late to do anything about it, is the decorative value of honesty evident in the garden. There are several seeds per pod and innumerable pods per plant, and the seeds are taken on the wind to end up in a cluster at the nearest windbreak, where they can start a colony next year. If you do not want them there, they can be extracted by the handful very conveniently. Those that get away greet you at every corner of the garden, even flourishing among the ground cover.

Of dahlias I had no experience, nor of the different varieties, so chose only for colour and texture. I love the tight little ruffs of the button variety which remind me of Tudor court costume, and the brilliance of the reds against a sombre purple. By mistake I planted some dwarf singles at the back of a border, and was sad not to see more of their clear lemon-yellow and velvety-red. Fortunately for my dahliascape, they were in the terrace bed and the taller ones by the back door, so the slope of the hill made the ultimate effect less disastrous than it might have been.

Without forethought it is easy to be beguiled into buying too much of the same colour. Red and orange are delightfully gay but by the end of the first summer I longed for some blue and was pleased to find that some Michaelmas daisies, both dwarf and tall, were more blue than purple. Several plants of *Campanula carpatica* had been put in along the edge of the terrace bed but they were too sparse at that stage to help very much. This was an area where I learned my lesson about having to wait a year or two before the plants merge into a mass. Now they are satisfactorily bordering the bed.

Looking up the garden from the gate, the fiery colour scheme was really noticeable that summer and the phrase 'a riot of colour' actually had some meaning. It is not a good thing. There is nowhere for the eye to rest, and if the foliage is green and unvaried too, very dull. Grey-foliaged plants like *Cineraria maritima* and santolina, together with purples like *Rhus cotina* and *Acer palmatum purpurea*, alleviate the monotony and tone down the harsh impact of primary colour. All are there now, and the mixture is much improved.

As well as being an uncontrolled mass of colour, the plants

struck me as a sheer jungle every time I arrived with a fresh eye on the scene. It had seemed so necessary to cover up that bare gravel-coloured earth, and now it was covered, but not satisfactorily. So plants were moved around in their due season.

Perennials were chosen at the outset of furnishing the garden, and only later did it occur to me that evergreens would be even less bother. Perhaps it was as well that this came after the teething troubles of arranging lesser subjects, as I can see now that bad mistakes can be made in choosing and siting evergreens and greys. The end product could easily be a display of foliage with small and insignificant flowers. A mixture—but the right mixture —should be the aim.

Every gardener will acknowledge the debt owed to the producers of glossy and not-so-glossy catalogues for the information to be extracted from them, once one gets the hang of things. The glossies are out for your money and appeal to the green suckers like myself, until they know better. The less brilliant but more informative ones are ready to make a friend of you for life, and if one feels mean about sending for one after the other when they are announced in the gardening magazines, the reward comes when, having received the order and set out the plants, you later prowl round the garden thinking 'Oh yes. That came from X's. They said it would be 2ft high and to leave 3ft distance between plants, and they were right.' I found also that although I might not be wanting to buy heathers, for instance, the moment I received a lovely catalogue full of them, at a later stage, when it was obvious that a peat bed would have to be made for two rhododendrons given to me by Father, I would have to consult the catalogue about some underplanting which would suit the acid soil requirements of rhododendrons.

Mere descriptions of some heathers can stir the imagination without illustration. In fact, to see bouncing masses of heather in bloom put me off at first, until I saw some tiny plants at a nursery and realised how varied and colourful their foliage can be; their flowering period is, after all, limited. Who could resist them?

Catalogues from specialist firms are the best, I believe. Hilliers, the Winchester firm who grow so many kinds of plants, have separate nurseries devoted to certain groups and issue separate catalogues about them, and from this you get the best of all possible worlds. There are many other comprehensive growers who come into the specialist category: Notcutt's of Woodbridge, Waterer's of Bagshot and the St Brigid Nurseries of Topsham, near Exeter, are ones which spring to mind. Quality and reliability are the keynotes of their existence and their catalogues reflect this. Justifiably there is a charge for the more instructive productions, and for the glossy coloured ones which cost a lot to print, but lists of plants are generally free, or available for the price of a stamp. This makes me feel less of a heel sending for a catalogue out of interest only, not intending to buy but merely to assess the firm's standard as far as possible.

Dwarf conifers and their related bedmates, heathers, are the current fashion in the gardening world, but do go to the specialist and not to the chap who adds a few of the more popular of these to his usual list to keep his customers up with the Jones's. The selection is necessarily confined to a few of the fastest-growing conifers as the seedlings or cuttings take years to develop into anything that looks worth buying. This is why even three-year-old trees, tiny as they may be, are relatively expensive. A firm which can afford to plant out land with a series of 'tinies' and care for them until they become saleable is more likely to provide sound stock for your garden than the non-specialist, who may be far more interested in other areas providing a quicker turnover of profits.

There must be many more specialist firms worthy of mention, but I have found the Wansdyke Nursery, Hillworth, Devizes, Wiltshire, to be the best suppliers of dwarf conifers. The owner, Mr H. J. Welch, an acknowledged authority on the subject, has written a most erudite and fascinating book on these plants, *Dwarf Conifers*. Also D. W. Hatch at Heath End Nurseries, Farnham, Surrey and W. H. Rogers (Chandlers Ford) Ltd, Eastleigh, Hampshire, specialise in dwarf conifers. C. G. Hollett at the Greenbank Nursery, Sedbergh, Yorkshire, sends beautifully packed first-class heathers, primulas and other hardy plants. His catalogue describes each type, is very well laid out and printed—a great pleasure to use.

Sunningdale Nurseries, specialising in ground cover plants, azaleas and rhododendrons, has Graham Stuart Thomas at its head, with books to his credit on the many different facets of his horticultural knowledge. *Plants for Ground Cover* was my bedside reading for a long time. The catalogue from W. E. Th. Ingwersen, Birch Farm Nursery, Gravetye, near East Grinstead in Sussex, is only inviting to those who know something about plants and know them by their Latin names. Tucked away in the very heart of the countryside, the nursery is a pleasure to visit; very professional, selling perhaps only little twigs of some special stock, but almost guaranteed to do well because in the initial stages the plants have been so carefully tended. The Bodnant Garden Nursery, Colwyn Bay, Denbighshire, is famous for its ornamental shrubs and trees among other things, and its catalogue makes good reading.

The late Margery Fish's East Lambrook Manor in Somerset has a nursery where many of her stock of unusual plants may be found, and Mrs Desmond Underwood of Colchester specialises in grey-foliaged plants. There are many others, but from this you can see that many a fascinating hour can be spent by the fireside just planning your dream garden.

One catalogue which listed tools after the plants, and other equipment after that, ended up with an entry on a hammock. It seems they had their priorities right.

Numerous large conifers have stood in the wells at the back of the car, or lain in the boot, while I attended carefully to my

driving so that they were not harmed. The moment they are out
of the car I can't wait to get them into the earth, after the usual
careful preparation with peat, silver sand and a lot of water.
Arriving at the cottage with several specimens in containers, I
move them around among the existing plants until colour of
foliage, texture, etc are right. Having already checked on any
special requirements the new plants may have regarding position,
soil conditions and so on, I then dig the holes and view the plants
as they will grow at ground level. This is important as they
have quite a different appearance later when planted, and often
the glossy black or green containers influence one's views.

I cannot bring myself to order large plants for delivery by
post, but small ones, especially from Hollett's Nursery at Sedbergh,
arrive beautifully packed. It pays anyway to collect from local
nurseries, partly on account of climatic conditions being the
same, and partly so that you can select the best. This is not
necessarily the largest of several on show, but should be chosen
for compact growth, good foliage and a general air of well-being.
Smaller plants often actually transplant better than the larger
specimens, and quickly make new growth. Another advantage
in self-selection is the avoidance of postal charges, now becoming
prohibitive.

Chapter 8

Further Education

NEARLY two years after I had first seen the cottage, a plan of its garden planting was needed because in my new-found enthusiasm I kept buying things for the same spaces, because they looked attractive and healthy. When they were taken up to the garden there was often nowhere suitable to put them. 'A sunny, sheltered spot' the gardening book said, but there is a scarcity of these, so the plan made me cater for specific gaps in the planting. The diary begun in a very staccato way in the previous year was now amplified to note flowering-times and the peculiarities of plants I did not know very well. Also, I found that things 'disappeared'. Suddenly I would remember that a tiny veronica had been planted on the edge of a fairly sparse bed, and months later, looking for it at some distance from where it really was, would think that it had sunk without trace. When the plan was instituted, it made everything a great deal easier to keep track of and it carried over into the office working-week the interest of practical work at the weekends. It also taught me the lesson of scale, and the value of mass planting. The diary and the plan were therefore complementary.

A large peony had grown bushy and had covered up the veronica in question, so I did the best I could to give the little thing light and air and resolved to move it later. Having forgotten it in the press of other work, imagine my delight three years later, to find a mass of the delicate flowers flourishing despite the vigour of the peony.

There are many different kinds of veronicas dotted about, and following my mass-planting system, I shall gradually reorganise them together on a bankside, where they may be better appreciated. *Veronica pageana* (*Hebe pinguifolia* 'Pagei') at present about 6in high, but capable of being shrubby and twice as tall, is a delightful glaucous-foliaged plant with some upright and some semi-prostrate stems bearing small whitish-blue flowers at the tips. *Hebe armstrongii*, also shrubby but with whipcord-like stems of close-set leaves, bears white flowers like stars at the tips of the stems too, and with the dull golden colour of its foliage is really a remarkable plant. Where hebes begin and veronicas end I doubt whether I shall ever sort out. *Veronica incana* is an even greyer-leaved specimen than *pageana*, with hairy thin lanceolate leaves with slender spikes of very intense blue flowers. Another brilliantly coloured veronica is *V. prostrata* 'Lodden Blue', the many-flowered spikes drifting upwards all at the same angle like so many swaying dancers. *Veronica lyallii* has very delicate white flowers with tiny thread-like pink veins the length of the petals, giving them a dainty, crisp look. *Veronica satureioides* has these more abundantly and of a deeper pink; and there are lots more to be discovered.

The joy of being able to continue my gardening activities in London by the making of a planting plan and the keeping of a diary has already been mentioned. Needless to say, this was extended by the planting of seeds. All the tomatoes for the last three years have been hatched on the windowsills of the flat. Then that excellent part-work *Encyclopaedia of Gardening* came out, attractive from the first from a professional viewpoint, since I am a graphic designer, typographer and print buyer. Thus began my homework, and although after that publication the weekly gardening periodicals left much to be desired on the design side, at least there is something new to be learned each week from an article or a reader's letter; and now that the design is progressing, one gets the best of both worlds.

About this time Geoff, a great gardener friend, suggested a visit to the Royal Horticultural Society's show of the moment, which featured dwarf conifers among the daffodils and auriculas. He had gone to see the auriculas, and I thought at the time, 'That seems a pretty ordinary sort of plant for Geoff to be interested in,' little knowing what was awaiting me at the RHS show. Hurrying to the dwarf conifer stands, I was mesmerised by the great variety of colours, textures and shapes of these, and on my way out, dreadfully late for the office having spent twice my lunch-hour allowance, there were the auriculas. Some of the specimens with their mealy encrustations amazed me, and their unusual colours were enchanting, but one can only specialise in one thing at a time, and my thing-of-the-moment was conifers, so I admired the auriculas and passed on.

Now that there are a great many specimens in the conifer bed, I hope to find lots of time to explore the auricula field, for it promises many days of quiet enjoyment, and evenings of happy reading.

At this point perhaps I should confess to a failing: that of hating to get mixed up in a crowd. This limits many activities, and gardener friends cannot understand why I do not go to every RHS show, to Wisley, Savile Garden, Syon Park, the Chelsea Flower Show and many other points of reference for the serious gardener. This is where many of my readers will be able to upgrade their education on horticulture while Stay-at-home-Dougherty plods on regardless. There is no doubt that many mistakes might have been avoided had I had first-hand knowledge of the look of a plant or a tree at the outset; and equally little doubt that such knowledge might well have been acquired in all or any of these places.

Having elected, however, to substitute books for the real thing except when this is to be found where there are few people, I found that the books fall into several categories: those which are easy to read and exude their author's enthusiasm—in the main, specialist books; and those which are readable but rather less informative than those intended mainly as works of reference. In the reference category I would put such tomes as *Complete Gardening* and *Everyday Gardening*, both edited by C. E. Pearson, *The Amateur Gardener* by A. G. L. Hellyer, and T. W. Sanders' *Encyclopaedia of Gardening*; and in the former, easy-to-read category *One Woman's Garden* by Elizabeth Coxhead and that delightful book by Edward Hyams with photography by Miles Hadfield, *English Cottage Gardens*. Then there are the books which help us to identify plants—for example, the *Dictionary of Garden Plants* by Roy Hay and Patrick Synge, and Keble Martin's *Concise British Flora in Colour*. There must be hundreds of other books equally as useful as the ones listed at the end of this book, and many more specialist ones in fields not yet explored, so the list can only be a guide for the beginner.

These are the books which incited me to press on with the hard part of gardening by holding out the carrot of beauties attainable with a bit of patience and more knowledge. Did you know, for instance, that established lupins and broom dislike being moved and show it by dying on your hands? They have to be planted out in their permanent positions when quite small. And do you know which plants have shallow roots and so resent the use of the hoe near them? Do you know what time of the year to prune and how to do it properly? And do you know that some plants will not thrive in an acid soil, and some will not live without it? Basic stuff, but essential for the well-being of your garden.

One of the advantages I enjoy is working at The Design Centre in London's Haymarket. Here there are, from time to time, displays of garden tools and equipment. Many happy hours have been spent dreaming about new purchases: the sort of greenhouse that is made of almost indestructible material and would be a pleasure to work in and to keep clean and tidy (not just a tumbledown potting shed); the spade and fork which delight the eye as well as fulfilling their functions, feeling balanced in the hand; and many other things, not least, well-designed garden furniture—but NO GNOMES. Here also one can see a small selection of useful books which will perhaps attract you to a subject or to a facet of gardening not yet explored. As it costs no more to make things of good shape and colour rather than bad, there is real joy to be had from using well-designed and well-made articles, for whatever purpose.

New garden centres are opening frequently, as more people become interested in gardening. Their greatest value seems to be in making a wide variety of products instantly available locally, and in enabling customers to assess the merits of probable purchases against those of a similar kind and to notice the differing prices. You can spend quite some time browsing along the shelves finding all sorts of 'patent medicines' for diseases in the plant world of which you have never heard before. The garden centre is a super-super-market, and unless you are stronger-willed than I, you will emerge with a full bag and an empty wallet.

If you have time enough you can go from centre to centre and discover by comparison which of the ones nearest you sell the best plants at the most competitive prices. I have been put off buying things I very much wanted in garden centres (as opposed to nurseries, you understand) where weeds grew high among the stock and every container held not only the plant of some poor mug's choice but nettles and thistles and other weeds. One I visited showed immaculate sections of greenhouse plants, and what I thought were immaculate areas of container-grown plants, until I roamed round the back of a tall stand of conifers. There I found fruit trees and roses not, as first appeared, ready for the bonfire, but with price-tags as high as elsewhere, battered and full of weeds, and with a salesman encouraging an ingenuous young man to buy one of these poor bedraggled specimens.

Well-run nurseries are a pleasure to visit on any days but the weekends and public holidays—but that is my foible, and says nothing against the places themselves, which are interesting the year round. I recall spending a pouring wet day at Notcutt's in Woodbridge, wandering round in gum boots and a plastic mac, cursing the rivulets of water that ran down my neck and into the top of the boots, but happy as a lark looking at the name tags of

plants I'd never seen but had read about. In the end a trolley was nearly filled with purchases and the assistant remarked that it was a rare sale for a wet day. Probably he was thinking that it was not every day that he met such a fool, but since he didn't say so, we were both happy.

The power of observation contributes tremendously to further education in gardening: observation of other people's planting schemes, even though you may not wish to copy them; of the development in other gardens of plants you are thinking of buying; of friends' methods of propagating cuttings and dealing with seeds. It helps too towards an awareness of landscaping (as it is so grandly called these days, as though we were Capability Brown himself reincarnated), looking with a seeing eye at natural arrangements of foliage, texture, colour and shape.

From this you will learn that breaking up large areas of little interest enlivens a view. Natural 'obstacles' like big trees or small outhouses may be right in the way of an otherwise splendid vista. If, for one reason or another, they cannot be moved, breaking up the larger area with paths or beds invites exploration, and gardens within the total garden may open out to the visitor as he wanders up the path.

Experience has shown me that talking to plants, cooing, congratulating, admonishing, cursing, gets response from them in growth and flowering. Hospital treatment when necessary, even to splinting the damaged tip of a macrocarpa, pays off. You can become a good plant doctor through reading articles and books on your special favourites, and can guard against winter losses by taking cuttings in good time. If you don't need them later on, they can be given to the local sale-of-work, or to an old-age pensioner who may be delighted to add to his stock without cost.

Aftercare is important when a plant is newly introduced into your garden. It may have come from a site in totally different conditions, though it is to be hoped that you will have checked up on its basic requirements: acid or alkaline soil, sun or shade etc. Some good nurseries show all this on the name-tags attached to the plant sections, as well as such useful things as ultimate height and girth, flowering time, and most important, flower colour.

It is important to get plants into the soil as quickly as possible after delivery. Fortunately on only one of my hostessly weekends did I have to crave the indulgence of my guests while I sweated away under the summer sun to find a shady, moist part of the garden to heel in some little trees. And it made my heart bleed to stand gossiping with my neighbour when some rose bushes I had been given lay on top of the coalshed after being grubbed up. As soon as was decently possible in the conversation, I had to reach for the watering-can to push some of them in for a drink, and finally put the rest into a bucket of rainwater while

the planting holes were prepared. As the gift had come out of the blue, it took some time to decide where to put them, but they must have appreciated my rescuing them from hot sun and drying wind, as they have bloomed well for the last two years.

Even when moving plants from one part of the garden to another, I am careful to prepare the hole first and water it well, then dig up the subject, protecting its roots as it is carried to its new home, even sheltering some of the tinies in the palm of the hand. It is perhaps this aspect of gardening that fascinates me most—helping plants to grow, ensuring the right environment and treatment. I feel like a dog with two tails when cuttings are successful, plants are moved without casualties and invalids recover.

Patience is required for good gardening; if not inbred, it is soon acquired, or you are no gardener. The neighbours say that I have 'green fingers'. These figments of the imagination are a synonym for taking care, time and a great deal of trouble when planting out seedlings and container-grown plants as mentioned above, so that they have the best possible start in life in your garden. Shrubs and trees must have a large enough hole for the full spread of their roots, unless you are dealing with a 'balled' plant (one that has been lifted in the nursery in sacking tied round a ball of earth and roots for minimal root disturbance). Peat soaked and mixed with the soil at the bottom of the hole helps to encourage formation of a mass of tiny root systems from the main ones, enabling the plant to extract the maximum nutriment from the new surrounding soil. Good drainage and sufficient continuing moisture at the roots are necessary until the subject is established. If you are planting a large shrub or tree, staking before the roots are covered and a good firming-in are vital, because damage can be caused by wind-rock, and the plant is at risk until its roots are well knit within the soil.

It is pointless to put new plants into tired old soil and expect them to flourish. Sites should be fertilised well in advance of planting, humus should be added to sandy soil to give it bulk, and to clay soil to break it up. After planting, protect from the wind by making a shelter of wire-netting in two layers with bracken or other large foliage sandwiched between them, or with sacking and stakes or whatever similar material comes to hand. It may take a long time to rig up, but it pays off in the end.

Moving or planting out has to be done at the right time of year to succeed. You need a spell of damp weather (so that the plants are not straining to extract moisture from a hot dry atmosphere) in the spring after frosts have gone, or the autumn when the soil is still warm enough to help the plants get rooted and to give them a good start before they face the winter.

Watering sufficiently cannot be over-emphasised. Water the bottom of the hole, even when it has recently rained, earth in the plant, water some more, to help to settle the soil round the roots leaving no air-pockets, fill up the hole and firm in, then loosen the surface of the ground around the plant and water again. A two-gallon can of water, preferably rainwater, is not too much for most small shrubs. From this you will see how important it is to arrange good drainage before you even start to set the plant in its hole, so that, although the moisture is retained long enough for the roots to absorb all they need, any excess drains away. After all that, no green-fingering is necessary, only routine care.

There is a lot of incidental knowledge which comes in handy sometimes. Moles were making their presence obvious by a track of little brown mounds of earth criss-crossing the garden and threatening the roots of some of the choicest plants, so an expedition to the nearest garden centre resulted in a container of 'mole doom'—an unpleasant-looking black substance that had to be poured into holes made at intervals in the 'runs', which were then stopped up again with earth. Fumes are supposed to deter the velvet rodent from visiting the area for a long time. It is also said that moles cannot bear noise, and this has been proved by mowing sessions which are more frequent in summer than in, say, a damp autumn. The moles, freed from the racket of the two-stroke passing overhead just as they were thinking of coming up to see what the weather is like, dapple the grass with their earthworks in autumn and winter, but retreat, presumably to the belt of trees at the top of the garden, when mowing starts in summer.

There is something you should know about making bonfires too. Far be it from me to offer advice on how to make one burn —a bigger dunce at this activity it would be hard to find. I actually have to use a firelighter, one of those solidified paraffin blocks, before mine will even produce a decent curl of smoke. But wild life likes the remains of a bonfire because it is warm, and if you are in the habit of lighting one fire on the remains of another, do stir about a bit with the garden fork before lighting up. There may be a hedgehog or a frog or toad lurking there, hoping your big feet will take your enormous body out of sight and leave him in peace. This lesson I learnt the hardest way of all, by spearing a beautiful toad on my fork as I turned the old stuff up on top of the newly lit fire. He must have been doped with the smoke or surely he would have leapt to freedom earlier. The sight of him spitted on the outer tine of the fork made me nearly sick, but there was only one thing to do, so apologising profusely to him, I dealt him a death blow, and cremated him.

One further aspect of education in the sphere of horticulture is the language. Of course it is not necessary to learn all the Latin names for things, but if you do, you quickly learn more about the things you see at nurseries and garden centres, because a lot of these long names explain something about the plant. *Acer palmatum atropurpurea*, for example, is a palmate-leaved shrub, and those leaves are purple. Plants are classified into families according to the formation of their floral parts, petals, sepals, stamens, seeds and so on. The family Rosaceae, for instance, contains many other plants besides roses, including hawthorn, apples and japonica. They all have similar flowers, stamens, etc.

Families are divided into genera. All roses belong to the genus *Rosa*; *Malus* (crabapple) is another. Within each genus there may be several species—specific names differentiating one kind from another. This is a much more accurate way of discussing or describing plants, as there can be no doubt exactly which species of a genus of a particular family is meant. Common names are not so accurate, as many different names can be applied to one plant, even varying in different parts of the country. Once having taken to the more precise Latin nomenclature, you will be surprised to find that to know the species of a genus could save you from buying a deciduous plant when you thought it was evergreen.

Each species is capable of several varieties relating to minor differences like colour or leaf formation. Species can be grown from seed and the seedling can reproduce true to type, but some varieties grown from seed will not reproduce their exact characteristics, and have to be reproduced from cuttings or offsets.

It took quite a lot of uninformed reading for it to dawn on me that many varieties are designated by a person's name—the one who first produced that variety; for example *Chamaecyparis pisifera* 'Boulevard'. Among the heather catalogues I found a beauty: prostrate Mrs Ronald Grey. Properly it should have been described as *Calluna vulgaris prostrata* 'Mrs Ronald Grey', but that catalogue-writer had cut a few corners too fast.

And that reminds me that to be able to recognise plants by their Latin names in catalogues helps the liaison between armchair selection and actual buying. There is quite a difference between *Primula sieboldii* and *Primula denticulata*.

Chapter 9

Overstocked

FOLLOWING the intensive education from magazines, books, nurseries and garden centres on the subject of flowers, foliage plants and trees, I wanted very much to see some of them in the Suffolk garden. In my usual precipitate way no planting plan was prepared before a great many of them were bought. The plan mentioned earlier was purely an after-the-event arrangement for the convenience of identification, since I have a very short memory. I would go to a nursery fully intending to buy just one or two things, and get so enthralled with the many lovely plants about which I knew nothing except that their appearance was delightful, that I ended up usually with many more than could be coped with. This meant nose-to-the-ground sessions of planting out against the clock, not good garden policy at any time and never to be recommended for planting out. This is where I hope to be able to help readers to steer clear of trouble. There must be many like myself who want 'instant' gardens, not because we are not able to wait to see the full life-cycle of plants but because we get bitten by a sort of bug that makes us covetous and desperately curious to take the plant home and put it where it can be examined and its development watched.

Nose-to-the-ground tactics are liable to be disastrous. If there is one thing essential to good garden design, it is to stand back and take a long cool look at what you have there already, and at the possibility of rearrangement so as to incorporate one or two extras in which you are particularly interested. Do not do as I did, and look around for a space to put this and that (although with *some* regard for their likes and dislikes) and gradually fill up every corner. This is the sort of trap into which any beginner can be led by the urge to cover the soil. I do not altogether regret having done this, although I realise that unless swift moves are made soon, some of my favourites will be stifled by more vigorous growers. The stimulus of seeing a flourishing garden full from an early stage has to be weighed against the necessity of discarding or replanting a year or so later. One needs above all to take a balanced view of things, and to be prepared to throw out the less worthy subjects when they have fulfilled their function of filling out the beds until the better specimens grow larger.

It was surprising to see how much the growth rate of all plants was affected by the weather and evidently by the soil in this area. Only two plants out of some hundreds which were planted over the first two years have failed; and some which looked nearly dead on arrival after catalogue buying have picked up wonderfully with the minimum of treatment (remember that I am only a weekend gardener). My curiosity was undoubtedly the worst enemy of any garden design. To some extent again this has proved worthwhile, though looking across my garden purists would say 'Good Heavens! Everything but the kitchen sink!' Well, I planned to have that too later.

One of the inevitable results of 'impulse buying' was the extension of the cultivated part of the garden further and further from the house. The poor little house was now neglected and fewer visitors were invited, because they absorbed my gardening time. Although I love the surrounding countryside and look forward to the time when I shall have the garden well enough in hand to be able to spend some time exploring, that time is not yet. The terrible story of neglect can be assessed when I tell you that only after being in the house three years did I get round to

Page 101 (*left*) A simple and good-looking seed self-watering system. Made by L. R. Hite of Cambridge, these pop-up pots gave a high, 78 per cent germination of auriculas; (*right*) An Ali Baba jar in terra-cotta by Henry Watson's Potteries Ltd

Page 102 (above) Well-designed plant containers by Mouldcraft
Products; (below) New style in plant protection made by Duffin
Containers Ltd from Polyfulte (extruded box-sectioned corrugated
plastics) with 10-gauge-aluminium anchoring legs

painting the back door, and that was forced on me by a rainy day. After a bit of quick carpentry to keep out the wet, I could not bear to see the orange paint of the wood used for the stopgap against the green of the door. Since the rest of the house is painted pale blue and white, you may imagine what an eyesore that door had been to everyone but me. I did not see it—I just went in and out by it.

In a spot near the house huge bearded iris from my father's garden were planted, because they would be similar in height to the reb-hot pokers or kniphofias, as I have now learned to call them. Of course it did not occur to me until the iris started to appear in bud in April and were blooming gloriously at the beginning of June, that the kniphofias would not be seen until much later in the year. They do, however, look grand with the *Cineraria maritima* planted the previous year. I had thought that it was a low-growing plant, but it is now a splendid three feet or so. It has just been beheaded to prevent it getting leggy and to promote more lateral, bushy growth. *Santolina chamaecyparissus* also keeps throwing up additional side shoots with flower heads on them, but I am warned now. Previously the flowers had been left to open, and very insignificant they were too. During the autumn and winter, the plants became more and more straggly, but they were sheared over in early spring, and now, hopefully by being kept from flowering, they will fill out. The *Cineraria maritima* may be past this stage, but as it grew up over a week of rain to its present height, there is little to be done except trim to the height required or uproot it. Experience is gained by living with plants and letting them get past their prime, for the knowledge so gained is more likely to be remembered, and even subsequently applied to plants of a similar sort.

Across from the *Cineraria maritima*'s felty grey leaves are two *Rhus cotina* 'Notcutt's variety', with their wonderfully deep-red leaves. To see the sun shining through that colour is an unbelievable sight. The centres of the leaves are brilliant, translucent scarlet and the leaf margins deep crimson. The grey mass is a good foil for this and contrasts too with the tawny purple of the bearded iris and the light apple green of a large plant of *Helleborus corsicus*. That bed outside the back door is becoming more carefully thought out and balanced than most of the others.

One of my biggest mistakes was to fill the area under the apple tree on the terrace bed with plants which I scarcely expected to grow. Some of these will be moved; not without trepidation, since another move might mean their loss. As a precaution, some cuttings were taken when the right time came. *Convolvulus cneorum*, in late spring nearly hidden under the fading leaves of bulbs; *Acer palmatum atropurpurea*, which I knew from the start would have to be moved before it grew too big for its position, but was one of the victims of an 'impulse buy'; *Pieris floribunda, Pachysandra terminalis, Osmarea burkwoodii*, skimmia, *Euonymus radicans variegata, Choisya ternata*, box, golden laurel and Uncle Tom Cobleigh and all will have to be taken to other quarters and the area grassed over. This will provide a resting-place for the eye, a background for the back-door bed and an undemanding foreground for the heather and azalea bed on the far side of a lateral path. Additional bonuses will be the easier collection of windfalls and fewer broken branches of shrubs and flowers—though it is remarkable how they seem to dodge the worst of the fallers. Purist gardeners would be horrified to know of such a tight underplanting. All I can say in defence is that the yellow soil left by the builders cried out for cover, and in my greenest days it did not occur to me that grass, if kept in a trim state, would cover faster than any plants and be a great deal cheaper too.

In making the rearrangement I shall be careful to avoid too stereotyped a design. The whole garden has evolved from just those two paths trodden by the builders beside their trench, and although there is room for improvement in varying the colour of leaf against leaf, texture with texture and so on, I would hate to end up with the sort of garden conjured up in the mind's eye by overheard conversation between two office accountants on the way home one evening, discussing their probable activities. One could just see the neat little rows of rose bushes all well pruned, and the salvia, lobelia and alyssum edgings to the paths. OK for some people but not for me, even in a suburban area with the conventional lawn surrounded with flower beds. Thank goodness some of the gardening magazines are now turning their attention to articles on unusual garden layouts with focal points, and movement of interest through the length and breadth of the area. Other magazines are helping by publishing articles on some of the show gardens, and those of historic houses. These, though perhaps we could not hope to emulate, still provide ideas which can be adapted to a smaller scale.

As for the heather bed, I know that some of the heathers will have to be moved when they begin to clump together satis- factorily. Some of the earlier ones set out, before I had enlarged the original idea to take in the whole of the area between the lateral path and the well, will be too short and will get lost under the more vigorous growth of varieties like the 'Springwoods'. For the most part, though, this bed was more considered than most and specific gaps catered for. I was particularly smitten by the prostrate and hirsute heathers, and the enormous variety of foliage colours, especially when set off by the rich dark brown-black of the sedge peat. Irish moss peat is said to be the finest one can buy, but I found that it took far longer to wet out than the darker sedge peat, dried as a mulch more quickly, and, worst of all, was pale brown in colour.

At the corner of this bed there are five azaleas, 'Mother's Day', from Woolworth's. In spite of the ridiculous name, the plants have done heroically. There is one in my father's garden now, growing in conditions not altogether suitable. The soil there is sticky and heavy in winter, but the azalea gives a profusion of bloom which could scarcely be equalled by my younger plants —but I have hopes of competing with that example, since my soil is light and sandy and only needs to be kept in an acid state.

It is said to be a mistake to mix azaleas and rhododendrons. This year I saw the truth of the statement, although when I read it it seemed pedantic. Some azalea colours are less brilliant and penetrating than 'Mother's Day' and others seen blooming in nurseries, but the point is certainly taken now, as the rhododendrons are swamped by the brashness of the azalea colour whatever the variety. As further underplanting for the rhododendrons at the back of the bed, I bought two beautiful dwarf rhododendrons from the Sunningdale Nurseries: an *intrifast* and an *impeditum*. Luckily they were put at the far end of the bed away from the azaleas, their blue-purple blending well with their larger brothers and not at all with the azaleas. The grey curve of the concrete path and the foliage of the heathers separates them nicely, especially as most of the heathers at the front are grey-green *tetralix* varieties.

Behind the azaleas are two sorts of willow. They need moisture, so had to be on this side of the hill. *Salix helvetica* is a lovely silky grey and *Salix repens* is said to be rampant and difficult to eradicate. It could scarcely be more difficult than the *Spiraea salicifolia* which was rooted out to make a space for the willow. No one will be better pleased than I if it fights to the death with the spiraea, which has very dreary pinky-mauve long-lasting flowers turning a rusty colour as they die off, when they can at last be cut away with a clear conscience. Still, the spiraea thicket, although decimated to make way for the willow and other things, forms a useful windbreak on the more bitter days of the north-easters.

As hardly anything remained in the garden from previous ownership, the whole bed is a typical product of my pioneering spirit. It contains just one plant of the several Unknown and Untried dotted about, which I pore over from time to time, when I remember where things are, or happen to be weeding in that area. One such is *Cornus canadensis*, put in one September and rewarding me in June with two beautifully precise white flowers and its red-green foliage. Near to it is *Gaultheria procumbens* and a polemonium which have not shown signs of movement yet have overwintered without hurt. A deutzia bought years ago is only just settling down to produce new growth and flowers, so it does pay to be patient. Two hebes, just as reluctant to bloom, have covered themselves in glory now, after many abortive summers.

One of the greatest thrills was to see flowers, in February, on a *Daphne odora variegata* brought back from Devonshire. It is said to be a tender shrub but I wanted it near the back window where some of its reputedly beautiful scent would be most easily appreciated. The bed there is in a corner between the window and a wall and gets a lot of wind in winter rushing round in a whirlwind. Not only has it survived that, but is still growing strongly and producing flowers after being resited at short notice.

In that windy bed *Leptospermum pubescens*, a myrtle with lovely opalescent silver-pink foliage, and *Ceratostigma willmottianum* were risked; and *Abelia schumannii*, said to be deciduous, has overwintered in its summer coat for me. Perhaps the label at the nursery was wrong and it is *Abelia* x *grandiflora*, an evergreen. This and the fact that the daphne flowered encourages me to think that the worst of the wind's power does not quite reach the bed but stays on the path, leaving its débris as evidence. Since an anti-cat rustic gate with wire-netting covering was erected, there has been less wind in this area so perhaps that gave the newcomers a chance.

So many plants were bought at the height of my enthusiasm to know more about everything, that one of the raspberry plantations near the house had to be removed. Clearing that raspberry patch was a good thing as couch grass grew abundantly among the old canes. And as this was being weeded one day, the idea of a shrubbery came to me, so off I went to the Stour Garden Centre to see which of the shrubs I had listed as desirable were available. That shrubbery turned out strangely. Of course there were few of the short-listed items but many others for which, for one reason or another, I fell.

The most incongruous in its present setting is a lovely *Picea pungens glauca*, a blue spruce, a really lusty specimen producing in spring charming light-brown leaf-buds which are gradually pushed away from the stem by the elongating leaves within the bud tip. This presently bursts apart, liberating a whorl of heavenly, bright, blue-grey needles of new growth. Around this conifer two rows of sage seedlings were planted out, for want of a better place to put them. They were allowed to flower to see what they would produce, and very handsome the flowers were too, a lovely deep blue-purple to contrast with the grey-green of the slightly felted leaves. Into one corner of the bed went a variegated holly showing dark red new growth at the tips of the branches. Further towards the middle went a *Hypericum moserianum* 'Tricolor', bright pink leaves with apple-green and white stripes; *Cotoneaster dammeri*, a creeping evergreen with white star-like flowers, *Potentilla fruticosa* 'Tangerine', disappointingly showing yellow flowers instead of the orange implied by the name; hyssop, whose bright clear blue flowers are a delight, although it turns out to be quite invasive; balm, whose yellowish leaves give off a scent of verbena if crushed, but is also a menace to less lusty plants; one variegated sage and one purple sage, their foliage making a welcome break in the rather dead grey of the common sage in the border; several smaller potentillas for ground cover, *P. alba*, *P. fragiformis*, *P. eriocarpa* (all lost now in the jungle of sage and hyssop); *Polygonum affine* 'Donald Lowndes'; *Veronica incana*, another much lighter grey-leaved plant; *Festuca glauca*, a bit disappointing as the tufts of pearly-blue grass harbour scraps of dead straw-coloured festuca; and as another peak in this rather ground-hugging shrubbery, a *Eucryphia* x *nymanensis*. I now know that it is useless putting *Cotula squalida*, a sort of milfoil, under sage, or the tiny potentillas under lemon balm, as the more vigorous plants shut out the light and air.

This is another draughty part of the garden, as the winter winds sweep across the escarpment, so I can only pray that the eucryphia establishes itself before being put to the test. It shows no sign of deterioration yet, though equally no signs of new growth. It is, as a friend of mine would say, 'just thinking'. An amelanchier, another Woolworth's purchase, has flowered beautifully every year since planting, but the show is over so quickly that it is pleasant to be able to turn to a euonymus on the other side of the path to see more bloom appearing.

The red-barked *Cornus alba* 'Westonbirt' is also producing a flower for the first time, and higher up the garden a carefully nurtured Tree of Heaven, *Ailanthus altissima*, is making good headway after it was decided to move it from too close proximity to an ailing but progress-making *Cedrus atlantica glauca*. This was started in a tub down in the paved garden at the same time as I planted a *Cedrus deodara* in another tub. The latter flourished and became so big that it had to be set in the ground, but the *Cedrus atlantica glauca* was rather spindly to start with and at first made new leaf only at the base. But it has literally pulled itself up by the rootstraps since it was moved from the tub and put higher up in the garden where it could die in peace if it had to or survive if it would.

Every week it was visited to see how it was doing; sometimes I remembered to feed it and in the summer watered it with foliar feed. Gradually the growth started to climb higher up from the base, but it was very doubtful whether the so-called growing tip would ever produce new leaves again. Some of the nearby buds turned slowly from purplish grey to the brighter glaucous colour of new leaves, and often, looking at that spindly tip, I wondered whether it would not, after all, be better for the tree if it were docked; but then I thought it might just make it, and went away with the pruning knife. The tree must have heaved a sigh of relief and tried even harder to please. At last, when clearly it could do no better, the tip was taken off and the quantity of new leaves since then is quite astounding.

Near to the patient, too near for later comfort I fear, is a *Chamaecyparis lawsoniana* which has grown steadily ever since it was planted five years ago. For the first time recently it bore a quantity of tiny cones, and this year was bright pink all over with them. At first I was aghast, thinking the tree had contracted some sort of rust, but closer inspection brought me face to face with another phenomenon of nature. In front of these two large chaps a *Tamarix pentandra* looks very fragile and pretty in the spring with its covering of pink, and later a deep-red fuchsia (the old resurrected one) and a *Caryopteris clandonensis* are set off by the foliage behind.

Two years ago a great many lupins and delphinium seeds were sown at random in this and an adjoining bed. The reddish-purple lupins and the pale-blue delphiniums, with one or two really dark ones among them, are so closely planted that they provide support for each other and break up the 'woodiness' of the other occupants of the bed. In fact, it was not until seeing the result of such close planting that I realised how much more effective mass planting is as opposed to the single specimens in which I had been investing over the previous years. However, it is no good mass planting something you are not going to like, or which will not grow in your soil, or would take up too much room (like a forest) so the policy of one-at-a-time did serve a useful purpose too.

There are two things to be said quickly, lest my critics take me up on them: one, that as plants grow from year to year, especially perennials, each will need more room so you must be prepared to weed out to allow for this growth; two, that my main reason for buying single plants, apart from the economic one, was the need to study and get to know their ultimate appearance. This applies particularly to conifers impulse-bought when in their fresh spring coats. One can get some idea of their probable 3-D size from reference books and then decide where they could be installed and in what quantities. It is a comfort to think that to some extent this excuses lack of planning, but then I wonder whether

I am ever going to have the guts to dig up my most precious specimens and risk transplanting them. Time will tell, and part of the job may be done naturally as plants die off.

It may be of interest to record here that the first plants which consciously and for the purpose of making a mass were bought more than one at a time, were heathers. Recommended minimum plantings are of three to five of one kind in a batch according to the habit of the particular heather. So the peat bed is well furnished, and like the other beds, will ultimately have to be thinned out as growth increases. I reckon there will be enough for two gardens now.

Chapter 10

Odd Gardening

THE garden 'map' was a great influence on subsequent planting. It showed up faults in the graphic design which, when considered, were also faults in garden design, the most glaring being the lack of relationship of one bed to another. (All this is in reference only to the back garden, which involved the major part of the effort, since the plan of the front garden was more or less predetermined and I was content to leave it at that while I experimented at the back, out of sight!)

I decided to stop the cultivated part of the garden at a certain point. A windbreak was needed there, because without one the winter winds would be certain death to many of the new plants in the lower garden. The *Spiraea salicifolia* at the side of the well had increased considerably over the years and was becoming an overbearing nuisance. When some of it was uprooted to make way for the willows, pieces with good roots were transplanted for the windbreak. Another clump had been savaged by the builders, who had thrown hardcore into the middle of it, leaving a horse-shoe with a gap on the lee side. The neighbouring cats had been in the habit of pushing in there for shelter. This clump, after reorganisation into a better shape, together with the transplants, helped to provide shelter for the lower garden, but more especially for the exposed area nearby.

The new windbreak was used as a boundary for the two top

willow

cowslip

Spiraea
salicifolia

Erica cinerea

thyme

beds furthest from the house, one of them a seed bed made some
time ago. There were many bonfires on the site at the clearance
stage, and noticeably few weeds grew there afterwards. It occurred
to me that the soil there was rendered sterile by the fires, and
that, if fertilised and fed, seed could be sown in the very fine tilth
produced by raking the ground level after the bonfires. Peat,
bonemeal and dried blood were added and it was left for some
time to 'brew'. Seeds were then sown, and they did so well that
it was used for this purpose for several seasons, the goodness in
the earth being renewed each year. It has the advantage, too, of
being hidden from the house and so it does not matter when
nothing but bare soil is to be seen. I tried marigolds, stocks,
delphiniums, lupins and fennel (just to see what it was like).
I was warned, however, to cut off the flower heads from all these
before they seeded or they would be all over the garden in no
time at all. The one or two I must have missed have proved that
point. Californian poppies, wallflowers and others have all turned
out splendidly with the minimum of trouble except for a little
extra watering in periods of drought.

Watering a long garden, especially an uphill one, is hard work
even if a long hose is available. The six butts installed around the
garden are a real boon, and a definite improvement on bailing
out over the top of an old tar-barrel left by the last owner.

Down the garden from the newly planted windbreak at seed-
bed level, is an area of raspberries, referred to earlier as being
the only surviving patch of these in the cultivated garden. The
patch is of a size convenient for making an unobtrusive netting
cage, using long canes joined by rubber 'Hortiballs'. These are
quite simply black rubber balls bored with slightly tapering holes
enabling one upright and two transverse canes to be accommodated at intervals around the area, and the netting fixed over the
skeleton structure. It is much easier, when handling netting, wire,
nylon or tarred string, to wear clothes fastening with a zip rather
than with buttons. Folding, flinging or rolling up netting other-

wise becomes a fight to the death between buttons and mesh.

Alongside the raspberry patch, with a path between, is the tomato bed. For several years the tomatoes have been a delight. They are the variety 'Sugar Plum', very tiny by comparison with those tasteless monsters in greengrocers' shops. Their flavour is incomparable, and each Friday on arrival from London, even when it is dark, I walk round as usual to see what has changed since I was here last. I am rewarded during the season by a fistful of the most scrumptious tomatoes ever (the first crop the more so, because I had never before grown a tomato in my life), and slake my thirst on them while pondering on the future of a line of macrocarpas set as a sight screen to shut out the neighbouring corrugated iron shed and outside closet. All the old rubbish of years was collected on that shed roof—two wartime tin hats, bicycle wheels, bits of wood, basins, everything you can imagine. I willed those tiny macrocarpas to grow up quickly, while sucking my tomatoes or gathering a handful of raspberries before the birds could get them next morning.

'Amateur' tomatoes were then grown from seed, but by force of circumstances and lack of time, the seedlings were leggy when planted out. Last year the site was changed as too many crops of the same kind is not good husbandry, especially with tomatoes. These got off to a poor start because a young lad who was helping me then was asked to put fertiliser round the plants. Since he had said that his father's tomato plants were twice the size of mine, I assumed that he knew how to deal with them. When I looked later to see what he had done, I found the fertiliser heaped up round the stems of the tiny seedlings instead of spread out and lightly forked in around the perimeter of their roots. A greener-than-green gardener, I concluded, as the stuff was hastily raked away from the stems.

Another earlier factor which affects the well-being of tomatoes is how they are handled. Avoid touching their stems when planting out, holding them only by the leaflets. The first two

years I had religiously adhered to the rule when planting out
'Sugar Plum', but this time I was in too much of a hurry to get
the seedlings in, and the results were not so good.

At the end of the early-tomato bed was a small lilac tree which
trickled water down my neck as I went up the path on a rainy
day. For this reason it was cut hard back, and after that began
to die off, eventually being cut down and used for firewood.
Regrets followed because it might have been saved had I known
something about pruning then, and had it been well watered
during the long hot summer that followed its beheading. However,
a rowan replaced it, set well back from the path this time, to
avoid drips down the neck. Since then, further thought having
been given to the ultimate spread and height of a rowan, it has
been removed to a more roomy position.

After this, reference books were consulted on pruning. One or
two salient points emerged, the most obvious being the reasoning
behind the knife or whatever you use. The objective is to encourage new growth by removing old, dead or diseased wood; to
remove reverting growth on variegated plants, ie plain green
shoots on golden privet or the variegated forms of ivy; and to
retain shape.

Then at a nursery I learned that some shrubs and trees never
need pruning. At that stage, being still unsure of my skill, I asked
for information about amelanchier, *Choisya ternata*, *Rhus cotina*,
elaeagnus, azaleas and rhododendrons, leptospermum, daphne,
eucryphia, mahonia, skimmia, pieris and pachysandra before
buying them on the assurance that no pruning was needed.

Sometimes a shrub or small tree needs trimming to keep it
shapely or to check its growth. An abelia made a lot of straggly
shoots one year and these were carefully pruned away. A couple
of berberis, intended as a rather formal filling to one side of a
bed, had to be trimmed a bit, and ribes, the flowering currant,
falls about all over the place unless given attention from time to
time. Escallonia can get a bit out of hand too, and rosemary,

which sprawls in its fragrantly spiky way away from the prevailing winds. Someone told me that vaccinium should be pruned, but mine is still so small that it gives no trouble. The viburnums, on the other hand, are much more vigorous and do need checking occasionally.

It is much better to take the trouble to consult a reference book if in doubt about your latest choice specimen, than to rush out with saw, knife or secateurs, like a surgeon performing an operation blindfold. One *can* learn from experience, as I did with forsythia, cutting it down to size ruthlessly the first year—and in the autumn too—only to find no bloom at all the following spring. No wonder, since the potential flowering shoots were cut down along with the old wood. The invaluable notes in the diary reminded me the next year where the mistake was made, and I now know that it should be pruned straight after flowering so that next year's wood can mature throughout the summer. Usually, when pruning is needed, it should be a regular annual event, like spring cleaning.

Of course one drawback to my system of close planting is lack of access to individual shrubs for pruning. Straining at an awkward angle to make a cut often means a break which then has to be cleaned up, or a cut in the wrong position in relation to a bud. So your roses need to be well spaced, and the forsythia should be well away from the skin-lashing cortaderia, or pampas grass, and the ground cover should not be of a kind to resent heavy feet.

The essential thing about pruning is that the cuts must be cleanly made. A ragged branch must be tidied up with a very sharp knife, otherwise it is disease-prone. Tree pruning, carelessly done, often leaves one with a jagged stump after sawing off a large branch. A notch should be cut in the underside, which will then be met by the cut from the topside. It helps if branches are supported towards the end of the cutting operation, and big branches should be cut away in sections of a suitable length to support, not sawn off all at once. It is surprising what a comparatively small branch of a tree can weigh once you, and not the tree trunk, are supporting it. There is also the consideration of easy transport. Shorter pieces fit better into the wheelbarrow.

If a whole limb is removed, the final cut should be flush with the trunk and any raw wood over 1in diameter should be painted with Arbrex to prevent disease. There are firms which specialise in tree pruning, but do ensure that they know what they are about. Some people let loose door-to-door callers on their trees, usually for convenience or because they are persuaded that it is the right time of year, but these casual callers' knowledge of the theory of pruning is non-existent and their promise to 'pick up the rubbish tomorrow' is rarely fulfilled. Then one is faced with a charge by the local council for removal of special rubbish—that is, if you can get it removed at all.

A recommendation from a good nursery can be quite helpful to ensure the services of a reputable firm, and if you know something of what should be done and can put a few intelligent questions to the pruners before engaging them, you are well insured.

If a tree has to be cut down to a stump, it is as well to remove this as quickly as possible. The dreaded honey fungus, or bootlace fungus as it is otherwise called, invades with incredible rapidity, as the wood is rotten anyway. This presents a hazard to surrounding plants, as the fungus runs through the ground at a great rate and can contaminate plants almost overnight. There are preparations offered to make stump removal easier, though few in fact can truly be said to do this. Drilling big holes in a tough old stump well out of reach of my electric drill is not my idea of 'ease', but once the holes are made and the instructions followed carefully, the stump can usually be removed after a time by firing.

A decision about the likelihood of extensive future pruning should be made before subjects which dislike removal are allowed to settle in. The conifer plantation described in Chapter 13 has been closely planted because an immediate windbreak was

Page 119   (*above*) The heart of the welding together of the two gardens. Seen from the bedroom window is the concrete base of the now-demolished loo between the privet and the philadelphus, with the back of the boat bed in the first garden beyond. The shed on the left of the privet has now been removed; (*below left*) The bread oven nearly demolished. In the nick of time it was decided to retain the part farthest from the house wall and build it up to make a 3ft-high brick bed for alpines; (*below right*) Completed brick trough made from the remains of the oven.

Page 120 (*above left*) The sundial and star bed at first stages; (*above right*) The paved garden rediscovered and the terrace bed developed. Now the sundial squats happily among dwarf conifers in the star bed; (*below left*) The same viewpoint as the photo on page 49, but here the paths are laid, and pampas grass, marguerites and the foliage of a large philadelphus give a more cared-for look; (*below right*) The two houses seen from near the top of the first garden

required and the original 4–5ft shed-screening macrocarpas were regarded as expendable when other choicer specimens demanded space. However it is important to remember that the slower-growing shrubs and trees will need extra attention to avoid all nutriment being absorbed by the larger trees.

With pruning in mind, ultimate spread *has* to be considered, or some specimens ruthlessly removed to make way for the up-coming plant. The ability to get at it from all sides, coupled with its own demands for light and air, dictates planting space, and if you are willing to keep down the weeds inevitably covering the ground until the ultimate sizes are reached and several seasons' leaf fall have covered the intervening spaces, then take note of growers' instructions on planting intervals. It is a straight choice between instant effect and ultimate good.

The words 'instant effect' spark off another train of thought: that despite my haste to get the conifer plantation ready, it was a fascinating exercise in arrangement for effect, not dependent on blooms at all, but achieved with a wide variety of foliage types, and several different colours, shape, height and spread. Juvenile foliage is very attractive, especially in conifers, and other plants, shrubs and trees may be kept effectively producing juvenile foliage by pruning. *Eucalyptus gunnii*, some forms of variegated or yellow-leaved shrubs, weigela, philadelphus, or even lilac if you don't want any bloom, add freshness and colour to the garden. The formation of berries and other bright fruits in the shrubbery depends entirely on the good management of pruning, as the flowering shoots produce these ultimately.

The correct time for pruning is often difficult for the beginner to sort out. I do not pretend to be expert at this at all, but the lesson of the forsythia always sticks in my mind. Winter jasmine and philadelphus are others needing the removal of flowered shoots, and it is obvious that if this is done as soon as the flowering season is over, a novice can tell which are the flowered shoots. Leave until later, and it's nearly impossible.

In the main, plants in this early-pruning group flower up to the middle and the end of April, depending on the geographical position. Deutzia, philadelphus and weigela, which flower in early summer, have puzzled me for a long time. Their new growth has been made by flowering time, yet they flower on the matured wood. Therefore to get bloom next season, one must avoid cutting out what seems to be a lot of pushy, overcrowding new foliage, and shorten flowered shoots right back to new growth, or cut the whole flowered shoot back to the ground, as it will be unproductive if containing only old wood. The centre of the bush or plant should also be opened out by removing thin growth.

With buddleia and *Caryopteris clandonensis* flowering during the summer until about September in East Anglia, pruning has to be delayed until spring as no new growth will be evident before then. Again I learned the hard way, having nearly killed my beautiful caryopteris by too much pruning at the wrong season. A really well-established, bushy plant is one haze of the most unusual blue—rather the same effect as a bluebell wood.

Evergreens rarely need drastic pruning and should not be touched until frosts are over, usually about mid-May. Any winter-damaged wood can then be removed, and the early-flowering ones treated as described for deciduous plants, their flowered branches cut back to new growth. So some pattern emerges, and as with most things, practice improves knowledge until the pruning tools can be applied without reference to notes, but with an understanding of the principles behind the job.

You may move to a garden where regular pruning has not been carried out, with the result that a poor show of flowers or foliage occurs in due season. I was lucky to come to my garden after only two years' neglect, but even that showed. Eventually I had to become brutal and cut most of the wood hard back, removing all the old wood back to base. Even though one season's loss of display may result, the general health of the plant improves, as with the never-forgotten forsythia. The following year should see a large degree of restoration, and regular pruning will improve a plant all the time.

There seems to be a great vogue for flowering hedges—roses, ribes, broom, cotoneaster, etc, and for laurel, berberis and shrubs other than the formal privet hedge which has contained so many suburban gardens for so long. Before planting shrubs as a hedgerow, thought should be given to the pruning aspect, otherwise there will be a good show for a year or two after the shrubs have settled in, but after that, without proper pruning, they will fall into decline. Cutting out the flowered shoots and dead wood in such a way as to promote growth to 'fill out' the shrubs is essential.

For more formal hedges, trimming is perhaps a better word to use than pruning, although the aim is roughly the same. Whether done with an electric trimmer, sheep shears or garden shears, the object here is to keep a good shape and to thicken up the growth for screening purposes. No hedge should be under-cut at the base or it will lose all foliage there, resulting in a row of bushes with gaps at ground level, like rotting teeth. The sides should be sloped outwards so that the base of the hedge, seen endways on, is wider than the top. In this way a greater expanse of shoots is given light and air and so the bushes thicken at the base. Young hedges especially should be kept trimmed to this shape to encourage basal growth.

Laurel hedges are supposed to be pruned with secateurs to keep their shape and tidiness, but I have often thought what a laborious job this must be for those having great stretches of laurel hedge. It is the type of hedging (as are the larger varieties of rhododendron), more often seen in big gardens. The idea behind not using shears on these shrubs is to preserve the leaves whole, but the comparatively few severed leaves soon wither and drop off. Holly is useful for hedging, not only because it needs little, if any, trimming, but is, with berberis, a prickly deterrent for straying animals.

Most hedges benefit from a final trim before winter comes, and

I do mine about September, or if the weather is unusually mild, even later. Some small amount of new growth may then be made before the really cold weather.

I suppose the elimination of suckers caused by too vigorous digging round plants prone to this condition can be classed as pruning, since each sucker must be traced back to the main stem and cleanly severed there. It is useless simply to pull the tops off, as this causes much more spirited sucker growth. Suckers form on grafted plants—roses, some shrubs and trees. It follows that suckers from the underground part of the stem are more likely to be from the original stock than from the scion (the grafted shoot for which the plant was bought) and so, if left, will drain the resources of the scion. Reverting growth will be made, with bloom to match. To discover whether new shoots from ground level are from the stock or from the scion, the scar made by the joint between the two must be identified and all new shoots below that point destroyed.

Just as sucker removal is on the fringes of the subject of pruning but included because the objective is the same, so deadheading, pinching out, and disbudding come to mind, as these are also directed to promoting healthy growth, removing dead material and retaining shapeliness. Disbudding is not an activity of mine, since the type of garden is not one where prize specimens, or single blooms, are cultivated. The removal of lateral buds at an early stage in a plant's life ensures that all the nourishment taken in at root level goes to the perfection of the single bud remaining. Chrysanthemum growers are great practitioners, and those grown by my neighbour show just how rewarding the fiddling job can be, if that's what you want to do with your time. Pinching out is a similar thing, directed more at unwanted side growth to promote filling out and the bearing of flower or fruit. This is often practised by tomato-growers.

One plant which needed no help at all in filling out was a lusty Russian vine (*Polygonum baldschuanicum*), trained along a fence topped by a trellis to keep out the cats from next door. They still took a delight in leaping from the flower bed below, up on to the stout tree-trunk uprights of the wire fence, and bounding through the diamond spaces in the trellis. Try as I might to fill these with vine, rose cuttings and other twiggy material, they always managed to move a piece to make a hole large enough to get through when they were being chased. I *wish* I liked cats. The kittens were absolutely adorable, but time-wasting with their antics and eventually far too prolific and destructive.

Two tall flowering plums (*Prunus pissardii*) with lovely rich red-brown leaves were planted against this fence, along with one in the boat bed to complete the group. When first planted they were about 4ft tall and rather weedy so between the two on the side bed two roses were planted, one of them the great 'Queen Elizabeth'. That just shows how green I was then. 'Othello', the other one, shrank back into the ground and would have died right off had I not decided just in time to move all the roses dotted about that area into the boat bed around the other prunus. 'Queen Elizabeth' was by that time scrambling up for light and air, but being the tough old woman that she is she was in good fettle when the time came to move her. You can be sure that those two roses got the pampering of their lives, being sunk into nice, deep moist pockets of sandy loam and peat. They showed their gratitude by coming up again grandly with a fine crop of blooms, and now I can get at them to prune them.

It never ceases to surprise me when plants respond to my amateur treatment, however firmly based on acknowledged authority. A bergenia has been completely revitalised by the breaking up of a large old clump when new shoots appeared after rather spasmodic flowering in the first year. Pieces of new growth with a good amount of root attached to each were broken off the main plant and put into moist leaf-mould and other compost, and watered in well. Spread about near the parent plant, not only have the new pieces taken root and flowered the following year, but the parent also has responded to the extra air and light. The lessened demands on her root intake resulted in lustier and more prolific heads of her bright pink flowers than I had seen before.

The same treatment should be given to bearded irises, but be careful after dividing the rhizomes from each other to replant them facing the sunniest spot and resting on a small mound of earth so that their roots are buried but the rhizomes get baked in the hottest sun. When the leaves of the flowered plant begin to die back, and these transplants are made, the remaining leaves should be trimmed down to a neat fan-shape. This helps to promote root growth by lessening the strain on the plant to produce food for the leaves. Some tall white irises which had not been doing too well in the shade of a big privet hedge and the apple tree on the terrace bed, have been treated in this way.

To continue our walk down the garden after my digression about pruning and other related matters, the space beyond the second prunus and before the rain-dripping lilac was covered with campanulas, sweet rocket and Siberian wallflowers. Although, to my surprise, these have a honey-sweet scent, I cannot say I care for their very brash orange colour unless a great deal of silver foliage tones it down. When sitting at the dining-table, one can sometimes see the sun shining through the brilliant crimson of the *Rhus cotina* leaves, against a background of this Siberian wall-flower-orange behind a clump of *Cineraria maritima*. On either side are conifers in tubs, completing the picture.

The sweet rocket was a wow! It grew on this side bed (as it had under the apple tree) to a great height and in a close-knit pattern of stiff lateral branches clothed in their dark green foliage which sets off so well the small, sweet-smelling pale flowers.

Further down the side bed is a passion flower which has been near death each year since planted. The first time this happened I despaired of its life, but noticed that there was a tiny new shoot emerging from the straw shelter given it for winter, although the rest of the plant appeared dead. This was cut away and the new shoot duly climbed up to the same height as the old one but late in the year; the first frost nipped its progress in the bud. Cut back again, I really gave it up for lost, but it struggled up once more. It would be better to move it to a warmer site, but the builders have prohibited the spot on the warm south wall for which it was destined, so I tell the little patient that it will have to keep going until I can find it a place in a better ward.

Pride of my heart is a *Euphorbia wulfenii*, bearing in early summer great heads of the typical euphorbia green bracts which appear to be the flowers. The real flowers are quite insignificant in the centre of the bracts. The foliage of this variety is dark blue-green, setting off the lighter bracts to great advantage. During the short time I have had it, it has grown bushy and tough, nearly 4ft high, and clearly benefits from the sun it enjoys for most of the day. After deadheading, a piece of charcoal rubbed on the cut stem will staunch the flow of white latex and so prevent the plant from bleeding too freely.

On the wall behind, there was a dark-red climbing rose and a pink rambler, but the latter was badly mildewed when I took over the property. Even though it was cast out, the mildew transferred to the red rose, so now they have both gone on the bonfire and the wall is bare and waiting for the next part of the building scheme.

In the bed outside the dining-room window, besides the *Daphne odora variegata* and *Leptospermum pubescens*, the climbing and rambling roses and innumerable bulbs which appear every spring, I found room for a beautiful dark-purple *Hebe speciosa* 'Autumn Queen' and a *Vinca minor* which will be kept cut back to form a shrublet. Here in the centre was the original transplanted rose which was saved from the first builder's path for the trench. This year it was moved again, out of the way of a second onslaught of builders. There will be even more sorting out to do in that bed. *Berberis stenophylla nana* 'Crawley Gem' deserves a better spot, but *Veronica lyallii* and *Abelia schumannii* together with the adenophora, two or three hellebore seedlings and the lovely *Ceratostigma willmottianum* which has brilliant blue flowers and pink-tinged foliage, can stay amongst the peonies, which hate to be moved about.

One more hellebore which I refuse to risk moving is one of the most beautiful flowers I have yet seen, *Helleborus orientalis atrorubens*. This was standing among others of its kind outside the packing-shed of a local nursery where I had already well overspent, but it was so perfect with its great purple flower heads delicately stroked with green to tone down the purple, almost to earth colour, and its handsome, large, dark-green, leathery leaves, that I simply had to have it—the collector again.

The boat bed, bounded by the builders' paths, forms the main feature of the lower garden and leads the eye towards the wood at the very top, and to the fruit trees between. It is planted with the prunus trees already mentioned and small shrub roses leading up to the 'bridge'. This is roughly where the second manhole cover comes, and the roses flow round this, leaving a pathway across it made of stepping stones and a dry stone wall round three sides of the cover to hold back the earth which would otherwise wash down the hill in wet weather. Rock plants are grown over this wall. There little *Veronica prostrata* 'Lodden Blue' are already rearing up their spires of bright blue and I look forward to being able to transplant two healthy specimens of *Polygala chamaebuxus purpurea* to spread their neat cushions of dark-green leaves and tiny prostrate dark-pink flowers in course of time. I must remember that they need an acid soil, and give them plenty of peat and sequestrene. A glaucous sedum is already spreading out in the sun, and there are many other suitable plants to be arranged there.

Behind the second manhole cover the centre of the boat bed, roughly amidships, is presided over by a pampas grass, *Cortaderia argentea*, just beginning to get going after some indecision. I was sharply reminded of a warning received, and promptly forgotten, never to work near this plant without wearing gloves. An innocent piece of what one thinks is couch grass becomes in the hand a two-edged sword. Although damaging my hand only slightly, noticing just in time what it was that I was grasping, a nasty cut can be taken from the leaf of pampas grass. The first year it produced several of those lovely feathery plumes which wave in the breeze like silk, but get so bedraggled if left on the plant too long. In front of this grand plant, a cluster of Californian poppies with their strong red petals around a seed pod bristling with thick black stamens, adds a welcome patch of colour to a rather grey area. There are pinks of varying depths which accord quite well with the red, for they are delicate and their centres are not black but a beautiful green, the petals shading to white near the centre. On the red poppies there are patches of black at this point, as though the 'mascara' from the stamens has run on to the petals.

The third and last manhole cover was completely hidden for most of the year by rank upon rank of white marguerites which grew sturdily until the little clearing in their midst was quite unseen. Their dark-green leaves are quite attractive while they are getting ready to flower, but these need regular deadheading or they look very untidy. Also the plants multiply very rapidly by offshoots, and an area can be quite overrun in a short time, so I had no qualms about uprooting and burning some each year. In a windy garden they need firm staking too. But now they have all been removed and I can use the paths again.

Behind these, in the stern of the boat, are two small philadelphus which were rooted from a larger bush in the paved garden. The smell of the blossoms on a June night is gloriously exotic, a cover for any less pleasant smell which may be around. Michaelmas daisies rise to carry on when the marguerites are past their best, and these surround the two philadelphus, by then back to foliage or twig. In the boat's wake comes a froth of candytuft grown from seed—another gesture of curiosity to see what effect a much lower-growing plant would have as a tailpiece to the bed, which I always regard as moving forward towards the house.

Chapter 11

Conifer and Heather Craze

THE main point of interest in the front garden is the steep banked driveway. One of these banks was already full of a motley collection of plants hidden under a cloud of field grasses, when I took over the property. These are very pretty but scarcely had their right place in that area. Patiently, week after week, the bank was weeded and weeded and weeded. Now only the occasional spikes stick up to make me blush. Most of the rock plants were left there, some because it was impossible to uproot them, so deeply had they dug for moisture between the rocks. Besides, there was plenty of more urgent work.

In the main, the bank nearest the house was clothed in St John's Wort, snow-in-summer, the biggest strain of grape hyacinths I have ever seen, wallflowers, tiny peonies which were often dug up inadvertently as I strove to tidy the bed, and aquilegias which have appeared in every possible place year after year, however religiously deadheaded. Since the north winds sweep with terrible force across the face of the houses, they are rather tall for the bank.

In winter, before I learnt how to wriggle the car round an old apple tree which stands about 6ft in front of the garage, I used to leave it for shelter at the entrance to the drive. There the banks rise on either side to roof level, but there is very little space for getting in and out. Since the weekend when friends Michael,

Margaret and their son Matthew were booked for a visit, and I knew that Michael would arrive proudly in his beloved Citroen and would not be happy to scrape the sides of his loved one against the rock, there have been wild schemes for widening the drive. I was right—he left the car outside, though that was almost as hazardous because the lane is very narrow. Perhaps that accounted for the brief moments of their visit.

They had come to see the inn sign which painter-friend Bryan and I had done for the King's Arms in Hadleigh. The landlord had invited us to be present at its unveiling, and as Michael was my boss, I thought he should see what other talents I had. We had a meal at an inn in Boxford so that they could see a little more of the countryside, and I had a ride in the famous Citroen, even being given a demonstration of its ability to raise and lower the body when we went through the ford at Kersey. I must admit to having given way to a naughty impulse in suggesting that my visitors could not go back to London without having seen Kersey. I really wanted to see whether Michael would get the car's feet wet, but had not reckoned on its being able to swim.

Widening the drive was not on, I decided, even for Michael, as the sumach planted with loving care the previous autumn was just coming on nicely and I was very hopeful that it might have some of those lovely purple spires on it in due course. At that time I was unaware that there was a male and female sumach, and that unless one had the right pollination, purple spires do not materialise.

The other reason for not wanting to move anything was that the only side where it would have been possible to cut back the bank was the one where the conifer collection had been started. This was, as you may guess, on the bank facing the house, because I wanted to see the evergreenery of it in winter. And not only greenery but yallery also, and the grey of *Santolina chamaecyparissus* and one or two of the conifers.

At first there was no intention of extending the bed on that

side as far up the driveway as the one on the other side, but only
to tidy up the existing bit of cultivation to match the state of the
opposite bank. But just then I made one of my rare visits to
shows—the RHS show of conifers—and saw all those tempting
little dwarf trees with their new foliage making them look enchanting. I took copious notes and wrote at once for catalogues.
The Wansdyke Nursery had shown most of those specimens I
simply could not live without, so an order went off quickly and
the plants came, in excellent packing, to the London flat.

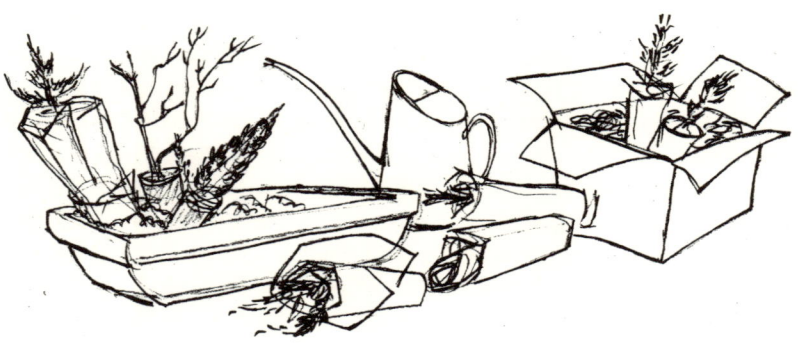

When any order is delivered, my first thought is to open up
the parcel and give the contents a drink, both through their
roots and over their foliage. I have several of those useful polystyrene troughs in which plants were once grown on the windowsills. Now they are used to harbour my latest acquisitions until
they can be taken up to the Suffolk garden and planted out. If
they were to be delivered to the house, they would not get their
drink as soon as they arrived. There is always a small bag of
peat in the flat, and a quantity of this is put in a trough to wet
through. Then, leaving the plants in their containers, pots or
moss, they are laid in closely to keep each other warm, and the
peat packed round them. In this way I have not lost a single
plant with a good root; though it was not possible to save some

little spindly things from another source, which were sold as rooted cuttings. They should never have left their mothers so soon, to be exposed to our postal 'service', and were nearly dead on arrival.

The bank already had some interesting sempervivums and saxifrages, though at that time I scarcely knew one from the other. They contributed a difference to the texture of the bank, the sempervivums bulky, formal and stiff, the saxifrages in flower reminding me of pin-cushions. Other than that, the all-pervading sedum which occurred in the back garden, and makes ground cover *par excellence*, clung here to perilous crevices and so acquired a suntan and was less lusty, and more attractive, than the more lush growth on flat fertile ground.

The top of the bank was weeded and a row of santolina, or cotton lavender, a grey, feathery-leaved shrub, was put in against the grass edge, to form a background for the conifers. The whole bed, then still only a few feet long and about 2½ft wide at the top, was peated and watered, and peated and watered until it was fit to put in the first few precious plants. At all times, but especially when dealing with conifers, it pays to try to cope with the Latin nomenclature mentioned earlier in the book. There are so very many varieties, all looking similar to untrained eyes, that the need for really specific labelling becomes apparent. Even so, those not used to dealing with conifers can easily get mixed up, and you may find yourself buying a fast-growing pine instead of a slow yew.

Previously the star bed in the centre of the paved garden at the back of the house had been prepared with the peat and water treatment and the santolinas when tiny had been set out there. Now they were too tall for the sundial but just right for backing up the conifers. In their place in the star bed went some tiny glaucous sedum for which I have yet to find a name, and some compact saxifrage—both of these at the tips of the star shape so that it could be built up in plant height to just below sundial level. The star bed and the front border of conifers were developed very much at the same time, some of the new plants being more suitable in scale, colour and texture for one position rather than the other at a particular point in their growth.

One or two larger specimens which I could not resist were planted in tubs: *Cedrus atlantica glauca*, until it began to look poorly and was taken to the top of the cultivated patch to pick up; and *Cedrus deodara*—two of these eventually, but the second was very small and droopy, looking like a forlorn child that nobody loved, so it was taken back to the flat to cherish. It did not look very much like my other, larger specimen, so I suspected its identity, but it turned out not to be an ugly duckling in the end. *Cryptomeria japonica elegans aurea* was the last. This goes a lovely red-gold in May after darkening to a deep greeny-grey in winter. The tubs were eventually lined up in front of the terrace wall to hide it until the aubrieta and other tumblers should have grown enough to do their job. Temporarily the larger conifer specimens stood sentinel to the tinies in the star bed.

Originally in the front border there was a very healthy clump of dianthus—old-fashioned white ones—which at first I did not want to move as the blue-grey spiky foliage contrasted well with the other plants. Then some more appeared out of the grass a bit further along, and a few Canterbury bells emerged, so there was a blitz and they were moved to other quarters and I continued the preparation of the left bank for conifers. A few weeks earlier a *Juniperus virginiana* had been planted rather at random, so this went into the bank with a nameless cupressus from Woolworth's, and the two complemented each other well. *Pinus mugo* and *Juniperus repanda* were the next arrivals. The pine had attracted me at the RHS show, its new growth like little green candles standing in dark-green saucers. Often I linger over it in passing.

Two thuyas went into the star bed—*Thuya orientalis aurea nana* and *rosedalis*—with *Juniperus* x *media* 'Blaauw' and *Chamaecyparis aurea nana* and *Abies balsamea* 'Hudsonia'. A seedling macro-carpa, the only one to survive in a batch of seed sown the previous year, and a tiny pine seedling which was a bonus with some heathers, were also found places in the star bed. This can only be a temporary planting since some of the varieties will make quicker growth than others: the macrocarpa, for example. But they are there at present because they fit the scheme or fill a space or both.

Juniperus sabina tamariscifolia and *Juniperus squamata* 'Meyerii' were later added to give a feathery blue-grey colour where needed. When they were first planted and for some weeks after-wards, all the conifers were watered regularly, and during the drought of that summer they were given a foliar feed once a fortnight. It was well worth the trouble as they have now settled in nicely and made more growth.

After that I started compulsively buying heathers for the peat bed of rhododendrons and azaleas: *Erica carnea* 'Springwood White' and 'Springwood Pink', *Erica darleyensis* 'George Rendall', white *Erica vulgaris* 'Hammondii', and *rubrifolia*, flowering in August and September—the first lot are winter flowering, and most of them are 18in to 2ft high. More peat was added to that bed and it was enlarged to take more heathers. That meant that three parts of the garden were developing simultaneously and on some sort of planned basis. It also meant that all my 'pin money' was going on the garden, but I had no regrets.

Chamaecyparis obtusa nana was the next arrival in the front bank, a lovely bundle of rich dark-green whorls like a dancer's skirt. A grey hebe was put next to this, partly to break the rigid line of grey at the back of the conifers, and partly to vary the grey by introducing a darker tone and a different texture, the tight little growing tips of the hebe making a good contrast with the light-grey feather-like growth of the santolina. This was just about to flower, and foolishly I let it do so, only realising too late that this puts all its strength into making the flowering heads and none into lateral growth.

I think the *Picea omorika* was a mistake. In the nursery these small Serbian spruces had looked slim and elegant with their down-drooping arms of foliage. Back at the house, the only place to put the poor little thing was in a patch dug out of the lawn behind the conifer bank, as it did not accord with anything in the front ranks. Since then it has made more growth and looks more at home there, but for a long time I contemplated moving it: but where?

The same problem arose when I fell in love with an *Araucaria araucana*—the monkey puzzle tree—and put that in the centre of the larger area of lawn in front of the sitting-room window. It looked plain daft, but now it is beginning to move so the decision may have been right after all.

A little golden yew was the next to go into the conifer bank, making a good contrast in colour with the others already established. In fact, it was my first 'gold' in that area, as all the others had gone into the star bed. In August the advent of a splendid specimen of *Juniperus pfitzeriana aurea* and *Chamaecyparis lawsoniana lutea* caused a great upheaval in the conifer bank, but when the dust had settled the arrangement was much better; the golds were spread among the greens and greys and, thankfully, not one of the plants suffered.

The bed by now was extending towards the house, but still it seemed unlikely that it would ever match in length the one on the other side of the drive. For one thing, it was convenient to get out of the car at the top of the slope and to be able to walk off on to the grass, not on to a planted bed. Later, when I was really 'hooked', this was not allowed to weigh in the consideration at all, and the bed climbed up to be the same length as the other, and looks all the better for being so.

I am reminded by my notes that earlier in August some small *Cineraria maritima* were planted in the star bed to add a grey element to the conifers and sedums. These were successful only

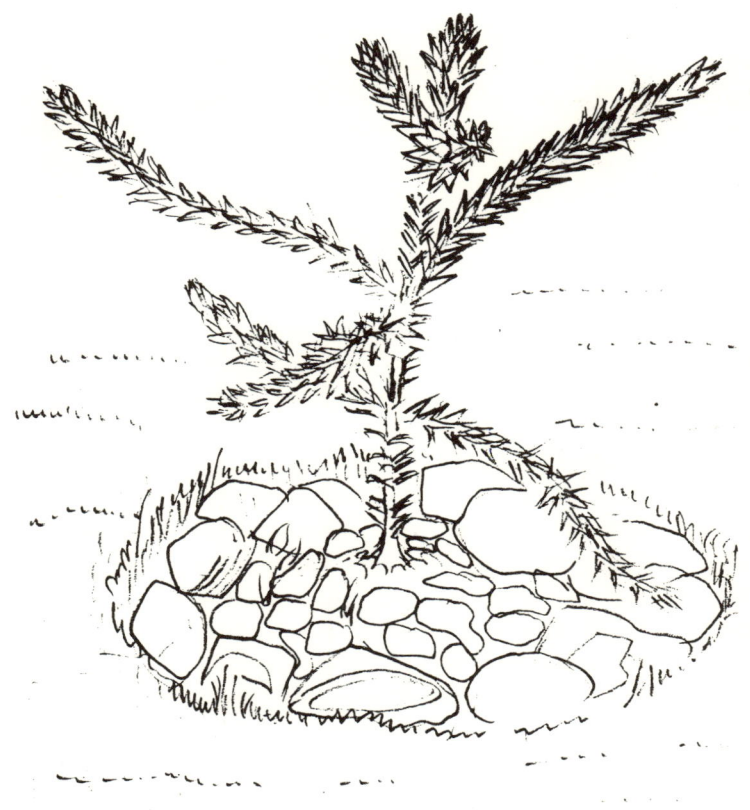

the monkey puzzle tree, Araucaria araucana

for a short time as they grew too large and overwhelmed the conifers, but the contrast between the deeply lobed, velvety leaves of the cineraria and the prickly-type foliage of the junipers and pines was very good. The two golden thuyas went well with them too.

Then followed a really naughty spending spree at a local

nursery, where there was a beautiful *Picea pungens glauca*—my most expensive plant, I think. It was simply asking to be treasured by someone, full of healthy tufts of pale blue-grey needles set off by the dark bark of the branches, and curiously twisted as though already a Bonsai subject. After much thought about displaying its beauty on the bank, I gave it more spacious quarters among the sage seedlings, as mentioned already. I cannot think that this will be its ultimate resting-place, but at least it can be admired without too great an excursion from the house.

Another yew—*Taxus baccata fastigiata aurea*—a tight column of bright yellow leaves looking so like a newel that it was eventually sited at the top of a little flight of steps up from the paved garden, joined the gang, together with *Retinospora nana gracilis* and *Picea albertiana conica*. These were the product of a trip to Devonshire with garden-minded Mary who inevitably took me to the local nursery. Needless to say, they were not the only purchases. Surely nurseries must have been the inspiration for supermarkets —in both places impulse buying must far outweigh premeditated buying, and impulse buying is largely stimulated by the visual impact of the product; thus the emphasis on smart new packaging and display in supermarkets, now being imitated in the garden centres selling fertilisers, containers, insecticides and tools, in addition to their far more attractive stock, the plants themselves.

More heathers were bought for the azalea beds: *Erica carnea praecox rubra* and *Erica tetralix* 'L. E. Underwood', a beautiful grey-leaved heather which went in near some hydrangeas in the peat bed, contrasting well with the fresh green of their simple leaves and with the dark blue of their big flower heads. *Erica vagans* 'Cream', a Cornish heather with bright yellow foliage, went in behind a blue *Chamaecyparis lawsoniana columnaris*, and it was then decided to furnish the rest of the conifer bank with heathers as ground cover. There, I felt, the plants should be kept as low as possible if they were to be preserved, so some happy hours were spent at the London flat with the catalogues. *Calluna vulgaris* 'Sister Anne', another one with grey leaves, *Calluna vulgaris nana compacta*, little bright green cushions, and *Calluna vulgaris prostrata* 'Mrs Ronald Grey', the most charmingly dwarf of them all, were ordered.

Then Mary and I visited W. E. Th. Ingwersen in Sussex and came back with a number of beautiful saxifrages: *Saxifraga aizoon pictiniana*, a charming little bunch of leaf rosettes with margins which appear to be studded with tiny white beads; a relative, *Saxifraga aizoon rosea*, which speaks for itself; *Sedum spathulifolium cappablanca*, very beautiful, plump, rosy-grey, spoon-shaped, velvety leaves covered with white farina, out of which in June come sturdy heads of yellow star-like flowers. These are more attractive to the plant as a whole when in bud than when in full bloom, I think. *Sedum glaucum*, a grey to contrast with the mossy mound of *Sedum lydium*, two artemisias, *schmidtiana* and *lanata*, and three *Europs evansii* completed the haul. The last group, the artemisias and the europs, are greys bought to make a change from the line of santolina as a background to the conifers, and to scale down to the end of the bank where the smaller plants were going in. The feathery foliage of *Artemisia schmidtiana* makes good contrast with the stiffer growth of the santolina and the broader-leaved, bluer-grey of *Europs evansii* makes yet another point of interest along the grass edge.

A visit to Alan Smith at Biggin Hill (a dedicated specialist if ever there was one) produced a number of sedums, saxifrages and really lovely specimens of sempervivums, which were all woven about the feet of the conifers. An unidentified cupressus from friend Robin's garden was put in too. The last was mentally christened *Chamaecyparis robinii*, but unhappily it suffered some root damage and has since died. Alas, poor *robinii*. In its last weeks it did, however, provide a lovely russet-coloured background for the long flower spikes of the *Saxifraga aizoon pictiniana*.

Suddenly, I had a yen for my namesake 'Bouncing Bet', a saponaria which germinated from seed under the worst possible

conditions and now foams like a billowing pink waterfall down the rock bank to meet some plants of *Saxifraga pectinata* 'Peter Pan' and 'Knaphill Red', and *Sedum rhodiola* (*Sedum roseum*), a lovely glaucous plant with neat little heads of yellow flowers.

Now some more little coniferous plants arrived from the Wansdyke Nursery and went into the star bed, causing some displacement there. You may imagine me like a demented duck, running round from one bed to the other with displaced plants, trying to find a suitable home for them. But this is half the fun of gardening. Perhaps the time will come when I shall know what to expect in terms of size and shape from most of the plants I get, and then the change will be dictated by perennials dying off eventually and leaving gaps. There are bound to be very good reasons why things should be shifted periodically, even if just for a change of face for the garden.

As an experiment in growth rate, conifer seed was sown, some outside in a seed bed and some in seed pans indoors. *Picea pugens glauca* and *Chamaecyparis lawsoniana* were chosen. Those indoors germinated more quickly and grew into bigger plants more rapidly than the outdoor ones. After one year, the indoor piceas were 2in high, with one little tuft of needles at the top of a rather spindly 'trunk'. The chamaecyparis had more foliage and were $3\frac{1}{2}$in high. Sowing took place in May, and in September the indoor lot were sunk in their seed pans into the seed bed alongside the ones which had germinated there. The difference in size was remarkable. Later the same year, after more growth was evident in the seed pans, one was broken up and the six seedlings transplanted to pots which were again sunk up to the rims in the soil, previously well watered. The roots in the seed pan went round and round the edges and were all intertwined. So much for the root ball I had hopefully thought to be able to transplant with the minimum of disturbance to a pot. They don't seem to have suffered though, and are still winning in terms of size. It is interesting to notice that those seedlings in pots sunk in fairly shady places in the garden are producing piceas of a bluer hue than those in full sun.

Of course the seedlings were well protected in the bed outside, and not only from the wind but from rabbits which invaded the garden and began to defoliate all the conifers. This was first noticed when, on my usual round of inspection, the *Cedrus atlantica glauca*, which had been moved from its tub and had made such excellent progress, was found to be almost entirely stripped. I nearly wept. Poor defenceless little thing, to have tried so hard to please, and to have been attacked so horribly. Oddly enough, all that was left of the foliage was the growing tip, so there was still hope. That evening I dashed from tree to tree, in order of my regard for each, fixing them all up with a wire-netting guard. What a nasty sight! But better than the fate of the cedar.

Then some of the front bank fraternity became too big: a *Picea pungens glauca* (not from my seed), another spruce and a fir. They were to go in gaps in the conifer patch in the back garden, and were most carefully protected.

Another major transfer of a cedar was now contemplated and my neighbour and his son enlisted to help. The larger *Cedrus deodara* was clearly outgrowing its tub, and although I had hoped to be able to remove most of the top earth before the chaps carried the tub up the garden to the tree's new position, this was found impossible because the roots were starting to emerge from the surface. So the two stalwarts actually took this immense weight up an awkward little lot of steps and up my bumpy beach-stone-and-concrete path, helped me to get it out of the tub and to settle it in the middle of the prepared spot. A very wide hole had been dug a week or two before and watered, fertilised, peated and generally watched over for weeds, and finally a mound made in the centre, on which to stand the cedar and to let its roots flow gently down into the earth. Not a bit of it. Those roots were so tightly wound round in the shape of the tub that I thought it best simply to leave them to sort themselves out. Buckets and buckets of water went into the hole, the earth replaced round the roots, and the whole thing netted against rabbit-devastation. Shortly afterwards, I was very pleased to see that the foliage was looking as usual, if not slightly better, and when spring came a great deal of new growth was made. Another liberated being.

Cupressus macrocarpa 'Donard Gold' made a fine amount of progress in the conifer patch, but was getting a bit straggly at the outer edges. These were trimmed lightly (and the trimmings pushed into prepared areas of the seed bed, where only ten out of seventy survived—but then, I didn't need seventy) and are now making much more compact growth. The brilliant colour of this macrocarpa will brighten any area and is a wonderful contrast with greys and greens. *Chamaecyparis lawsoniana* 'Stewartii' is almost as fresh a colour, and *Chamaecyparis alba spica*, if growing well and in an open position, will add variety.

Chapter 12

The Other Half

HERE even I thought a halt should be called, to wait and see how much ground all these plants covered and how much growth each made in a season. This pause enabled some necessary weeding to be done in the more neglected areas of the garden. Further peat mulches were applied to the heathers, conifers, azaleas and rhododendrons to keep the ground weed-free and moist.

By the end of the year relaxation was possible. After the full-pressure gardening programme of the last two years, the results were not exactly what had been envisaged but parts of it were pleasing, notably where similar plants were massed, as in the azalea, rhododendron and heather bed, the conifer bank, and the roses now massed at the sharp end of the boat bed. Another salient fact was that the planting was too dense in almost all the cultivated part of the garden, and I knew that thinning would have to be done when the due season arrived. But where to put the thinnings, which would not be the sort of expendables that lettuce thinnings are, for example?

Then my 'attached' neighbours moved out, and the vague notion of trying to raise enough money to buy the other half of the house crept into my mind. For weeks it was tossed around, taken out and examined from time to time, and thrust away again as being totally impracticable. Barely able to pay my bills now, how on earth was I likely to be able to pay twice as much in mortgage, if indeed one could be obtained at my present age, put the place in order, for it was in a lamentable state of repair, and continue with my job in London?

The other two houses of the four were having bathrooms and septic tanks installed. Once that had happened in the other half of my house, the price would be way above my head. It was a case of 'now or never', so I telephoned the owner to ask whether he was prepared to sell before the improvements were carried out. To my surprise he said he was, and named a price. So in I plunged, and once more set in motion the legal and building machinery for an application to the local council for a mortgage and an improvement grant.

Every time I walked up to the top of the garden and looked back at the house, it could be seen that as one property it would not only be more valuable but it would look so much better; and to contemplate what might then be done to amalgamate the two gardens was absolute bliss, even if the ideas were somewhat hazy. One thing was obvious—nothing would have to be spent on furnishing the second garden as here was the answer to my problem of overcrowding in the first garden. Plans could now be made for planting out with first-hand knowledge of the look and habit of the plants to be disposed in the second garden.

Totting up the cost of just the more recent purchases noted down, it dawned on me that becoming a compulsive collector was an expensive business needing a hard look and a lot of will power. I found that over £100 had been spent on plants alone in the past year, apart from fertilisers, peat, insecticides and tools. I now know a little more about the subject and can therefore buy selectively, no longer in the pioneering spirit.

While negotiations were going on for the house purchase, I watched with some horror a field of poppies, shepherd's purse, chickweed and all sorts of other weeds growing up on my prospective plot. Finally, the deposit paid and permission having been obtained, work could start in the new garden on things which needed doing to keep it in trim. Nothing radical could be done until the purchase was completed and the builder had indicated exactly where the trench for the new plumbing was to come, since it was to be joined into my present septic tank.

With a heap of work in prospect, the mind's eye view of the finished product keeps one from flagging, but I was really tired from the previous years' hard labour and decided that, for the time at least, some help would have to be sought to straighten things out. There was so much old iron lying about, so many weeds—another nettlebed, of course, as well as the field of poppies—and twice as much grass to mow. I asked Basil, my neighbour, for advice: would the boy who brought the papers be likely to help, and for what sort of wage? Finally, the boy agreed to come on Saturdays for a modest sum which I could afford for a while; and since he stoutly informed me at the outset that he would come until the football season opened again, I felt we were on the same wavelength, and Martin began to mow.

First we tackled the poppy field together. Everyone would have poppies if we did not cut the flowers down before they set seed. We took the tops off with a reap hook, followed by the Mountfield treatment as given to the first field of rough stuff.

Then the hedges needed attention. That was Martin's suggestion *before* he knew that there was a electric hedge-trimmer to play with. His initiative showed in many ways on that first Saturday. Most impressive was the way he would gather up the tools he had been using on the first job and put them together before he started another. He also had some constructive ideas when the mower broke down, although he said that he was not mechanically minded except when it came to mending bicycles. Deciding that he was capable enough not to cut through the cable of the hedge-trimmer, he was introduced to it, with all the usual precautionary injunctions, on his next visit. He told me, as he sat in the kitchen drinking iced lemon, that he was really enjoying himself; he must have been for he cut more hedge than I could have done in a day. Perhaps it was the novelty of the thing.

Later on in the hedge-cutting season he became so enthusiastic that he forgot there was an end to the cable, gave it a smart jerk to detach it from the hedge further along—and dropped the cutter hastily. It was soon in working order again, and when I said I would try it out to make sure it was safe, Martin said, 'Thanks. I didn't like that ole thing going fizz on me. I'm allergic to shock.'

Thinking it better not to leave him to be a 'single-handed gardener'—the ads for these poor unfortunate people always make me grin—but to treat him as a sort of under-gardener, I worked with him, making encouraging noises from time to time. He taught me several things during the first weekend: the difference between a blackbird and a starling, and the many other black birds there are around; how to tell wheat from barley and oats, which I had forgotten; but chiefly he taught me not to mind too much when he trod heavily on a clump of pansies in his efforts to please in some other direction. Soon I thought we might run out of jobs, except the recurring ones like mowing, which he seemed to enjoy as much as hedge-trimming.

Gradually, as we worked about the second garden and needed to get from one to the other more frequently, it was necessary to make a way through my cat defences. This was most easily done beyond the cultivated area, and we made a huge roll of the wire netting, leaving only the boundary wire for form's sake until the contract to purchase had been signed. In this wire we opened up a gap wide enough to get the mower through to the poppies and the wheelbarrow through to collect up the old junk.

Then there was the 'palisade' to take down. This was an erection of corrugated-iron sheets stood on their short edges and nailed to a wooden framework built up around a patch of grass where the children next door used to play. The thing had been an eyesore for years, and it was very satisfactory to see it come down and be put to better use as a shed for Basil at the top of his garden.

Every step we took to tidy up gave me a new slant on the possibilities of the other garden, but how to put the two together was still a mystery. I believe in letting the garden grow naturally rather than mine always being the master-hand. If a plant or a tree looks wondrous healthy and beautiful where it is, right in the way of some planned development, there it stays—as on a larger scale some motorways have to bypass buildings or trees with preservation orders on them—and a bed is created round it.

In the front garden, where I had planned a sweep of lawn right across the face of the two houses, there is a row of lavender bushes masking a drain-pipe which takes the water from the roof away from the house. Now that the dividing fence has been removed the lavenders form a nice clump and are so good-looking that the lawn now flows round them. That took some time and energy to organise, as the front garden of the second house had consisted of a straight path from front door to gate, where a neat *Lonicera nitida* hedge ran round the front boundary to a steep bank. At that point a pair of large ramshackle gates were asking to be replaced by something tidier, if not so solid. The local builder made these for me, and by outclassing the general state of the garden in that area, forced me to do something about it.

On one side of the path lay a rectangular flower bed edged with pieces of corrugated asbestos from some former structure, no doubt. A narrow gravel path ran all round this bed, which by the time I got round to it, was full of beautiful antirrhinums and huge grasses of all kinds by courtesy of the birds, I suspect. The antirrhinums were carefully separated from the grass and, together with innumerable bulbs of all kinds, were transplanted to other parts of the garden. The edging was removed with difficulty—asbestos breaks easily and if left in the ground would play havoc with the lawn mower—the gravel path raked and dug up, and the coarsest material fed into the pathway to the gate, as this was well below the level of the rest of the ground.

On the other side of the main path another triangular bed of plants and grasses was similarly dealt with, and became a convenient place to empty the grassbox from the mowing of what lawn then existed. I was in fact experimenting to see whether a satisfactory patch of grass could be made from a constant layer of these cuttings each week. The edges of that bed were steeply cut gutters, so there was a lot of infilling to do, and it occurred to me that growth and bulk would be assisted by peat and sandy earth. On the whole the experiment worked well, except that the rich growing medium thus produced was fair game for weed seeds dropped by birds or simply coming unnoticed in the grass cuttings. Chickweed was rife, and one or two clumps of barley, couch grass and other coarse material crept in, but these have now been almost eliminated. Some more work still remains to be done to achieve the level sward in my mind's eye, both there and where the front path was. This was brought up in height by digging the earth from the rectangular bed across to the pathway, since the former had been built up to quite some height over the years. When I thought the whole area was as level as it could be made, Lawn Carpet from Seed Developments Ltd was rolled out, covered with a thin layer of seed compost, watered well and never allowed to dry out. This handy pre-sown seed with a built-in safeguard against birds saves a great deal of time and heartache, though on my windy patch it had to be weighted down with bricks every foot or so, until the application of the compost helped to keep it in position. Even then it was essential to cover the edges and the ends well, as the wind gets under a corner and before you can turn round, several yards have bowled off down the slope. Eighteen inches wide is just about right for handling, especially round odd shapes, and it was interesting to notice the different growth rates of that covered with ordinary John Innes seed compost and areas which received a peat-based compost. The latter proved much more successful.

Alas, the old pathway which I had striven so hard to level off with the rest, was clearly consolidating lower down and the surface was about 1½in below the required level. It was about that time that I decided to cut out the grass from all round the brick bed in the back garden, so that the bricks could lie below the level of the lawn around, thus making mowing easier. This removal of grass was done by cutting turf, in a *most* amateur fashion. The turf was supposed to make up the path level in the front garden. Incredibly, the whole path has sunk again, and I now realise that with something like 18in depth to make good, every 6in should have been consolidated before more earth was added, instead of trying to do the whole thing at one go. Well, I'm a great one for doing things the hard way, simply by being too eager to see the finished result immediately. Now there is more work to be done there, to make good the level. But the grass is growing right across—it just needs to be higher. When really established the area will be cut round with a sharp spade and convenient amounts of turf rolled back, earth filling and fertiliser inserted, and the turf put back at a higher level than finally required.

The bank was a great trial. The first month or two it was lovely—full of bulbs, a very attractive euphorbia, snow-in-summer, blue geraniums, lupins, and at the top, as a screen to the rest of the garden beyond, a row of rambling roses which scrambled into the nearby trees and came to view again some way further along the bank.

'That will look after itself', I thought complacently, not then noticing the thin blades of tough grass thrusting up between the flowers. Be on your guard against complacency, fellow green-horns. A few months later there was little trace of the plants, now hidden under towering grasses, in themselves very attractive but not quite the thing to cover a bank such as I wanted. The remedy was to uproot carefully as many of the spreading plants as possible, disentangle them from the grass and replant them in a nursery bed for the time being, and then to cleanse the whole bank with Weedol and later with the Sheen flame wand. Even this drastic

Crested Dogstail

Field Brome

Catstail

Hairy Brome

Meadow Poa

Rye grass

Cock's foot grass

treatment has been only partially satisfactory. The grass is almost impossible to eradicate, and the bank is in such a position that any seed-drift from the crops the farmer sows in the field opposite and alongside are inevitably reproduced in miniature in the garden. That fickle wind again.

For the back garden no plan seemed to emerge. There were so many odd features to resolve: two old wooden sheds masked the view from the back window right to the wood at the top. They caused some heart searching, because if they were removed, the winter winds would slay the whole lower back garden. Then there were the two odd 'foundations', seen on the frontispiece plan. One of these actually had a shed built on it, but since sheds are costly things in prefabricated form, its owner had taken it away with him. Across a wide pathway, half hidden in the grass, more stone edging of heavier construction was found and the bed contained by it promptly commandeered for a tomato patch for that year, as it was well fed with sunshine the whole day and was a manageable area to dig over and plant out quickly.

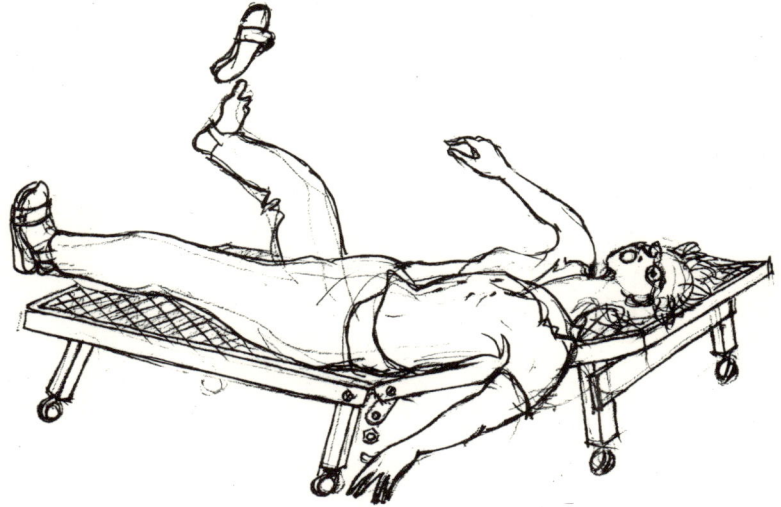

But how to weld the whole thing together? 'Give it time,' I thought, 'and it will all fall into place in the mind like the bits of decorating and furnishing of the first house.' And this has happened. Martin and I took down some more of the wire netting nearer the house and made a way through at the end of the old tough hedge. Martin cut some of this down expertly with a crosscut saw found discarded and rusty in the shed. We found other useful things here too: a folding bedspring now made into a proper rigid bed on legs; an old Windsor chair which was too far gone to cherish but was useful to stand on while decorating; two other quite respectable chairs which I could not afford to overlook with another house to furnish; and one or two other minor treasures.

Until the hedge between the two properties was right down it was difficult to visualise just what prospects there were. And there was more than just that short run of hedge to be removed. The builder had shown me where he wanted to dig his trench for drains, and this meant that several shrubs would have to find a new home. There were two lovely shining laurels, a *Cotoneaster bullata*, two *Prunus pissardii* with beautiful brownish-red foliage, and a shrubby honeysuckle, as well as the most prolific Russian vine.

All these were lifted in remarkably unpropitious conditions in August in a period of hot sunshine. One laurel was lost, no doubt partly due to my having stupidly planted it on the site of an old bonfire where I had found several torch batteries. What with the sterile soil from the fire, the contents of the batteries and the hot sun, I'm surprised that more of the neighbouring plants did not bite the dust. And once more I was staggering up the garden under the weight of a big tree. Like the fuchsia moved out of the way of the first lot of pipe-laying, the prunus trees had grown quite a lot and it would have been quite impracticable to load them on to the wheelbarrow. At last the way was cleared and other potential paths suggested themselves as Martin and I made our ways in and out from one garden to the other. The shifted shrubs made good after re-establishing themselves, clearly preferring the open light site rather than the pinched togetherness of the line-up along the 'cat-fence'.

While this was going on, Round Two of the negotiations for mortgage had begun. After all the shouting had died down I could return to gardening for the moment. At the back of the second house was a crumbling ruin of a bread oven which would have to be pulled down to free the whole of the house wall for damp-proofing in accordance with the terms of the improvement grant. Since it appeared to be very nearly down already, I anticipated not much trouble. I should have known better.

Although that small 5ft already broken cube of the old bread oven looked easy enough to knock down, like most of the other things I'd reckoned to be easy, it was really tough going. Martin helped tremendously, with energy and enthusiasm which might well have ended with a hole in the house wall, but we just

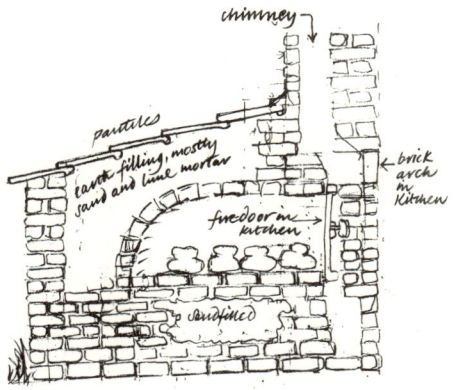

Fire made with faggots in oven before bread, was baked; ashes raked out and bread put in. Smoke circulated in oven, then up chimney (oven door open and recessed into chimney breast)

SIDE SECTION

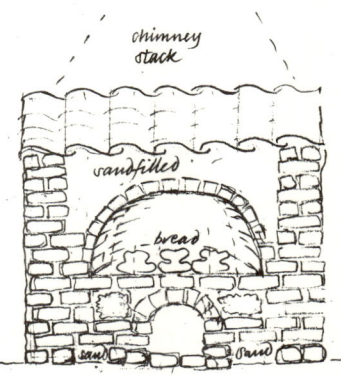

when building, a sand mould was made over which to set soft bricks for the 'crown'

FRONT SECTION

managed to wedge a loose brick or two in there in time. The chimney stack had been removed a year or two before, and the house wall was not very firm. Some bricks of the bread-oven wall had been keyed into the house wall and it was at those points where most danger of total demolition occurred. It took a whole day's work from two of us to get down nearly to the foundations. During that time I had been contemplating the relatively sound brickwork of the lower courses, finally deciding that if the builder thought the electrolytic damp-proofing of the bathroom wall would not suffer, I would retain half the oven base as a raised bed, making a concrete path between it and the house. The oven walls were full of limy sandy mortar, ideal as drainage material for saxifrages and sempervivums, and the little bed would get the best of the sunshine. It would also be high enough to enable my parents to take an interest in the tiny plants I had already put in there in my imagination.

Martin and I redoubled our efforts to find out what, if anything, was right at the bottom of the oven area. The results may be seen on page 153, drawn as accurately as possible from memory with some prompting from the builder, Clifford Tricker, who explained to me how it worked.

Having obtained the builder's agreement to the reconstruction of the part of the bread oven furthest from the house end, the wall was built up to complete the brick trough using some of the old mortar and new cement. The lower part was filled with as many stones and coarse open drainage material as could be found, then the old mortar, sand and smaller stones and finally a sack of good open compost. It was surprising how much was needed to get the final level up to the top row of bricks which formed the 'walls'.

Of course the incentive during all the hard work of building up walls and filling the trough was the pleasure to be had out of planting it up with the little rock plants bought over the previous weeks in anticipation of this moment. These were *Lavendula nana album*, a dainty dwarf white lavender; *Saxifrage cuneifolia*, two mossy saxifrages called 'Triumph' and another nameless one; *Oxalis adenophylla*, growing in close clumps with pretty pink flowers all over; two *Antennaria aprica*, enchanting plants with silvery, woolly foliage extending to the stems of the prostrate flowers, which open slowly over several days to a beautifully delicate apricot colour; *Penstemon pinifolius*; *Veronica repens*; and two very tiny conifers to make accents—*Chamaecyparis aurea variegata* and *Juniperus communis compressa*. There was also a tiny dwarf prunus donated by a friend, and to balance the silver of the *Antennaria aprica*, a small clump of *Chrysanthemum haradjanii*. This proved to be a mistake, since it must have been a very lusty specimen. It soon spread out over the surrounding plants and choked them to death. *Veronica repens* was not strong enough to withstand this treatment, nor were the one or two sempervivums put into the odd spaces. These made a great effort to get free by growing long thin stalks all pale and fleshy instead of well coloured and tough, quite uncharacteristic of their normal growth. The plants were surrounded with a good covering of small stones, with one or two really large ones for contrast.

Since the brick trough is a target for all the winds except a gentle southerly, yet receives full sun for most of the day, I hoped that the stones would not only keep down weeds but would help to retain moisture and keep the tiny plants in their places until their roots had a chance to develop. At the end of the day something had really been achieved which would entail the minimum of upkeep.

One reason for making special 'gardens', like a peat bed, an alpine bed, scree and sink gardens, is to provide special conditions for particular plants. A sink garden was planned from the moment that I noticed the shallow cream-glazed fluted sink which was to be discarded from the second house to make way for a smart sink unit. It was a constant problem to work out how it was ever to be positioned, but this was solved by Geoff who came one day to help, and quite simply hoisted the sink on to one corner and carefully bowled it over and over on its corners until we reached a previously constructed base in the little paved garden in front of the terrace wall.

There followed a time of experiment to ensure that drainage was perfect through the crocked sink hole, and that the rest of the sink bottom was well covered with drainage material. On top of the coarse layer went finer material which held up a layer of moist peat of the coarser variety, finishing off with John Innes compost. A bag of stone chippings was handy for the planting ceremony some time later. As with the brick trough, the whole thing was left to 'weather' for a while, in particular with the sink to ensure that the drainage plans had been adequate. Needless to say, the sink had previously been scrubbed with a Jeyes Fluid solution and all the crocks and stones making the basic drainage had been soaked in this, then soaked in a bucket of clear rainwater prior to use.

After that a happy long-time was spent laying the plants out in position and reshuffling until they were well composed in groups. After careful planting the surface was covered with the chippings and the waiting period began. At first all the tiny plants looked very isolated and the chippings very much in evidence. A year later it was necessary to prune and break up plants to save others being overcrowded. It was especially silly to plant *Gypsophila fratensis nana compacta* just behind *Sempervivum arachnoideum*, as however *nana compacta* the gypsophila is said to be, it is, after all, a trailing plant which completely covered the sempervivum until I spotted what was going on and put up an unobtrusive fence to save the attractive cobweb houseleek. *Geranium dalmaticum*, of a light-rose colour and 4in high, made a brave show. It is a neat plant used as a foil for a very tiny glaucous sedum given by one of my first visitors, who did not know its name, nor have I been able yet to identify it. Two comparatively slow-growing conifers were set in as spot interest: *Chamaecyparis lawsoniana* 'Ellwood's gold' and *Chamaecyparis pisifera aurea variegata*.

Campanula pusilla made a good carpeting plant. *Thymus serpyllum album*, said to be invasive, has not so far proved to be so. *Primula frondosa* in three groups was added later, together with a dwarf hypericum.

Stones are invaluable in these special beds, since they retain moisture in the soil beneath them. Collecting interesting stones for their colour, texture or markings, is a great hobby of mine, and the locality of the house greatly favours this activity. Flints of enormous size can be found on the hillside, often more than half buried, and many oval stratified-sandstone types as well as the more usual purples and greys and marbled ones which can look so handsome together or individually.

Tubs planted with specimen trees benefit from a covering of smooth stones which allow rain to penetrate between them while covering the root systems and keeping the whole tub moist and cool. The appearance, too, is enhanced by the right choice of colour and shape to set off the specimen.

The large flints, gathered on a special exploration of the unknown terrain at the top of the hill, nearly killed me getting them back to the house in the two inadequate bags I had taken to collect 'a few stones'. They are ideal for edging and holding up the bank in the new part of the garden, and have soon become a part of the whole miniature landscape, for that is what a gardener is creating in laying out each corner of his plot using natural resources at hand. The beach stones in the first paths made in the garden make wet weather quite a treat because it is then that the glorious colours in some of them are seen to best advantage. The more delicately coloured ones, carefully placed on the sink garden and the brick trough, help to hold back over-flowing plants and make a background for low-growing specimens which would otherwise get overlooked.

Stone of a different sort has been collected for pathmaking, and cinders each winter have provided the basis on which to lay the pieces in sand. As the paths are plotted a wider vista opens, and some young visitors voted it 'a marvellous garden for hide-and-seek'. I must confess to having enjoyed it myself. The area from one garden to the other where the trench had at last been made and filled in again, was now a bare sandy waste with a few plants remaining self-consciously awaiting their fate. Rainfall helped to settle the soil round the drainpipes, and gradually things levelled out. Once more an often-used preliminary track has indicated the route for a permanent path, and added interest to the garden inducing even adults (who do not play hide-and-seek) to explore.

The remaining part of the bread-oven structure which has now become the brick trough just described, makes protection for the lusty *Euphorbia wulfenii*, now grown to 3ft in height and more in girth in less than two years. All future plans for the garden have

adequate shelter as a first requirement. The short length of privet hedge leading to what was the old privy fulfils this function, as well as providing me with a basis for some 'fun' experiment in topiary. The general shape and bulk of the bushes reminded me of a large cow or a bull or an elephant. The subsequent clipping and-tying in of shoots has given me a little light relief from everlasting weeding and mowing though no doubt it would afford professionals considerable mirth. But at the end of the exercise, I was pleased to be able to have an excuse to retain as a feature something which friends had confidently predicted would be one of the first things to go, as the gardens were welded together. But then they don't live with the wind in this part of the land. This also gave me a further excuse to indulge my interest in conifers, which will be described shortly.

While all the renewed excitement of making sure that I didn't lose the second part of the house, and of planning the additional garden, was at its height, painter-friend Mary's life was slowly and painfully drawing to a close. More than ever the weekend 'escapes' were vital to retain a sense of perspective. In September she died; and ten days later, after a short spell in hospital which none of the family regarded as more than the usual routine check-up, my father died. He had no chance to sample the special arrangements planned for him in the other half-a-house, and of seeing the development of the first garden in which he had taken such an interest. Once more weeding, sowing and planting kept my sanity intact in the struggle to comprehend the double loss.

Mary's special memorial is a new window taken out of the previously blank wall facing the valley and Hadleigh. Something of the beauty of the view is to be had from the front windows of the house, but it is not until one climbs the hill to the wood at the top of the garden—roughly on a level with the bedroom windows—that the really superb view is seen, on the very side of the house where the wall was without fenestration except for a tiny landing-window.

When the wall was pierced to make that window, the builder found a brick inscribed 'Es. Sr. 1887', which he was careful to preserve for me. A small point, but it had always annoyed me not to be able to put a precise date on the house. There was the evidence.

With this window and some other improvements which were to come later, enthusiasm returned and ideas began to flow again.

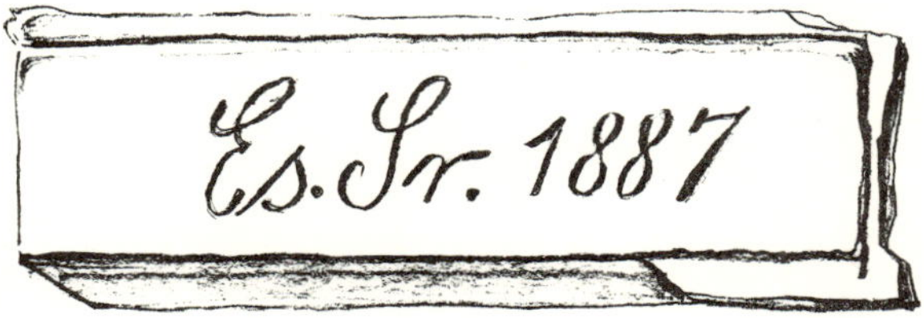
Es. Sr. 1887

Chapter 13

Full Steam Ahead

THERE could scarcely be a more difficult fusion of houses and gardens than those belonging to the four semi-detached cottages which make up Mount Pleasant. Each house looks out on to the neighbour's land, as the gardens all march up the hillside at an acute angle to the backs of the houses. It is a poor prospect for those whose outlook is on to a plot of shoulder-high weeds. And this unusual arrangement makes the two plots for which I am responsible more tricky to plan. It is a real challenge.

The second area is flatter than the garden of the first house, which sloped both sideways and downhill, but the flatter area is exposed to more of the winter gales. As a start, the rank of now well-established macrocarpas from the cat-fence line was moved into the open ground in the new part of the garden, to provide protection for the rest of the area. The patch where they were to go had been used for potatoes the previous year and so was in good heart. Certainly the rapid crop of nettles which replaced the poppy field thought so, but a large area was cleared and one after the other the ten trees were gently lifted and given the Dougherty-style treatment with plenty of peat under root. Unfortunately there was too much to be done elsewhere to ensure that they had frequent watering, but they were staked and given a netting screen to keep the worst of the wind off until they had established themselves and were making new growth. Unhappily

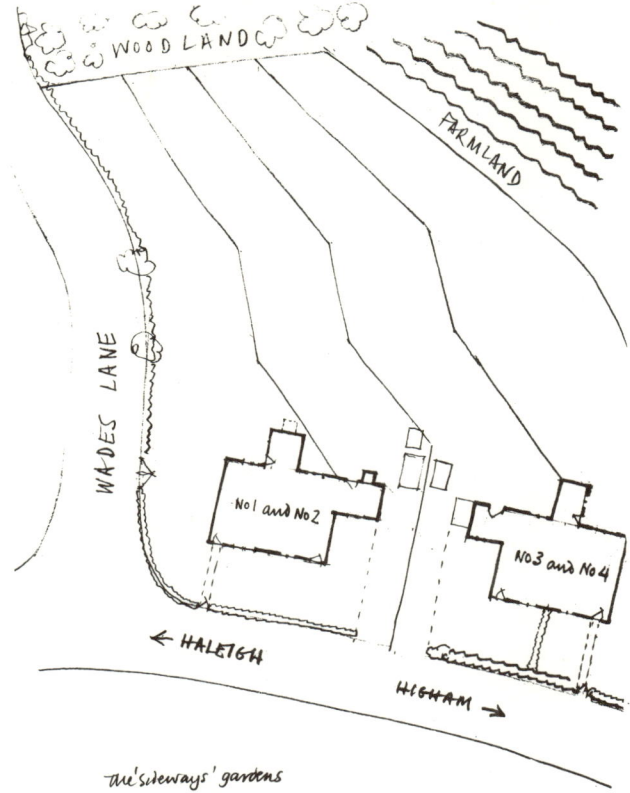

the 'sideways' gardens

one or two of them died in the process but I had anticipated this because they had lived a very sheltered existence all their young lives. Surprisingly, one set aside by the hedge, as being very dead but deserving a grave for having made a brave attempt to grow, was found two years later making new growth from the base. With the very dead leader and some other dead wood cut away, this macrocarpa is now trying hard to catch up with its mates.

Having sizeable trees of 4 to 5ft to set out gave me an idea of the ultimate appearance of the area when the dead ones were replaced, and the plantation really began to look satisfactory. The row of trees farthest from the house was lined up with the top of the cultivated area in the first garden, with the intention of concentrating effort in a smaller garden immediately surrounding the house, so that when I am older and less able to cope with all the land, at least the part in the vicinity of the house will be fairly trouble-free. With all the planting schemes, the accent has always been on evergreens and greys, hardy shrubs and perennials, ground cover and the minimum of upkeep. A mixed conifer group looks so much more lively than a 'set piece' or a row of trees for hedging/windbreak purposes. To plant very young trees in an exposed position, however, and expect them to grow to size on site is asking rather a lot. They do need some shelter until they are well able to fend for themselves. When they are 3 to 4 years old—depending on the type of conifer, of course—they should be planted out in their final positions. Planting older specimens is not recommended, although in these days of container-grown plants a high success rate is more likely.

Protection in their new quarters is perhaps not so vital where a group is closely grown with the idea of later 'weeding', but you may find, as I did, that the very specimen you most wish to preserve has succumbed, and a hardier but not so pleasing one will remain.

When planting out, I try to fill round the root tips with fine stone-free soil, and dig out a much larger area than the root spread so that the newly exploring tips do not have to battle through old consolidated earth just when they are at their most vulnerable. The root spread can be said to be roughly the same width as the foliage spread. I am always conscious of the damage done when newly exposed roots are allowed to dry out in the wind and sun (I have never forgotten those roses) and tend to be precipitate in planting, not stopping long enough to tease out properly the cramped roots from a pot or a container. There are two schools of thought on this practice, a fact which comforts me a bit: if the roots are too tightly bound together more damage can result from trying to prise them apart than from setting the plant into a well-prepared hole and letting it spread its feet at its own pace. Yet a well-spread root system helps to promote quick establishment and to keep the specimen on its feet, especially if it can be seated on a mound of soil and the roots allowed to flow downwards in a natural position to seek moisture and protection from the hot layer of topsoil. This does not apply so much to shallow-rooted plants, of course.

As the newly sited tree sits on its hill, and before the earth is fed round the roots, some of them should be gently parted and a good sound stake driven in between them. At an earlier, planning, stage I had to decide whether the macrocarpas and other conifers needed more than one stake, in view of the wind forces. Some of the larger trees were treated with diagonal staking, where a stake, driven in so that the top end faces towards the direction of the prevailing gales, is bound together with an upright stake before the tree is attached. Some of the very big ones had to have the 'wigwam'—three stakes set round at an angle so that they meet at a convenient point near the stem or trunk. Securely joined to each other, they make a near-impregnable set-up. Only my sandy soil could defeat them. Sand, however, is excellent material for filling in, because one can trickle it through the toes of the tree, water in, and be fairly sure no airspaces are left in which the roots can rot away for want of nourishment.

The other important aspect of planting out is that of tying up the tree to the stake. This should be done with soft and if possible slightly expandable, quick-drying material. What better than old nylon stockings? In my original innocence all the macrocarpas were tied in firmly with plastic string, a tougher, more immovable material than any other except wire. The latter is a disastrous thing to use for anything but annuals or plants where the stems do not expand in size for several seasons, by which time the prisoner's chains will hopefully have rusted away.

The trunk of a young tree will very easily get chafed and rot at the point of tying-in unless the material is soft and will dry out quickly. Even then the tie should be checked from time to time and if any swelling of the trunk is noticed, the tie should immediately be loosened or the tissues will be damaged irreparably. I find the figure-eight method of applying the tie works as well as any other more complicated system. There are, of course, special tree ties available in webbing, leather or plastics, but I'm for my tried and tested methods. They are cheaper too.

As an example of attention needed for newly planted subjects, I must relate the Tale of the Tall Macrocarpa. It was minute, and not expected to live, when set out with its bigger mates, but

wind-affected macrocarpas

in a short time, during which my attention had been diverted to quite another part of the garden, it must have found something very much to its taste in the ground—those potatoes perhaps—and the next time I passed that way, it had developed a lot of top-hamper and a list to port. I put in a diagonal stake, praying as I did so that the roots would not suffer too much at this late stage, and retired, satisfied that next time I saw the tree it would at least be upright. Imagine my dismay the following weekend when I found it much more inclined to starboard. Only a wigwam could now do the trick, and I cursed myself for having forgotten the lesson of the previous year's runner beans. The wigwam is the only certain staking method in my garden for plants which grow rapidly tall and dense.

In conjunction with staking and tying-in is the attaching of labels. Some people strip off the nurseryman's labels on planting out, preferring either to record elsewhere the often daunting official name of the subject, or to forget it entirely and wait simply for the plant to blurgeon forth so that it can be enjoyed for itself, Latin or common name regardless. I am all for the enjoyment of plants, but having a very poor memory and a real interest in the relationship of one plant to another shown by their Latin names, I am constantly annoyed to find the only permanent feature of nurserymen's labels is their own printed name and address. The name of the subject, often written on to the plastics label with a felt-tipped pen, washes off with the first shower of rain. Luckily my hobby of keeping a planting plan and diagrams for the diary has always so far saved the day, but it would be more sensible and better for the prestige of the nursery if the name of the plant were inscribed more permanently.

The anodised metal labels sold in two sizes are very useful for permanent record. Use an ordinary pencil, and the only way to get a name off then, if you want to re-use the label, is with abrasive powder or wire wool, both rendering the surface smooth and so no longer quite so workable. The labels are very convenient to attach to the stems, but if this is done too tightly and the stems swell in growth, one has to watch that the plant does not get strangled to death, as the label attachments are far from elastic. After trying sticking them in the ground beside the plant, and finding the birds' greatest pastime was to twitch them out and park them beside another plant, I decided to attach them firmly and at an easy angle for reading to a small stake set alongside the plant, unless the plant itself was staked, in which case the problem solved itself. I am much in favour of this type of labelling, though it must be unobtrusive. I am not likely to forget the appearance of the original garden at its earliest stage, all bare gravel-coloured earth stuck about with small stakes with metal labels attached. It looked like a graveyard, not at all like the forerunner of the jungle it has now become.

How long is a job? The timelessness of gardening is part of its therapeutic value. Staking and tying-in take a long while but are jobs to be done with complete concentration on what is best for the well-being and growth of the plants, gently moving aside foliage to get a tie in position, taking care where the stake goes and ensuring that when left, the plant is as secure and comfortable as you would make a guest in your house. There is no room for egotism or hypochondria.

So the gardening year rolled on, and the builders' rubble left by request was cleared up to make a pathway up the second garden to one of the shed sites mentioned in the previous chapter. One of the most difficult factors of this side of the whole garden was whether to retain both those oddly placed 'remains' or to make the prodigious effort of moving away the concrete foundations. By then the threatened football season had commenced (does it ever end?) Martin had ceased to appear, and I felt quite unable to cope with either the physical effort required or the mental one of how to treat the foundations if they did remain.

Making the pathway helped in the latter, easier, decision-making effort. There were enough bricks to build up a four-course wall on the shed site in front of the now enlarged conifer patch, and to make a reasonably wide pathway all round it. This had the effect of welding the wall brickwork to the ground and blending it in with the surrounding grass. At first the little walled area had stuck up like a sore thumb; just that additional effort made it part of the garden. Eventually the pathway bricks were sunk beneath the level of the grass, to make for easy mowing. When this was done, the ground exposed by removing the turf for the front path, described on page 148, was well treated before the bricks were laid with Pathclear and later with SBK when nettles still appeared. This proved to be a waste, as seeds blown by the wind or dropped by birds still lodged in the spaces between the bricks and had to be killed off in their turn.

Furthermore, from observation of the strength of weeds else-where, it would have been wasted effort and material to cement between the bricks, although it would have made them safer to walk on. It is so insensitive, too, in the context of a path or garden walling to use unsightly cement between bricks. So small plants, even the dreaded *Sedum album*, settle in the cracks and can be pulled away when they outgrow their welcome. Sedum makes for slippery walking in wet weather.

It is surprising how many bricks are needed even for the smallest thing. I knew that bricks for pathmaking should be stood on edge, but could not imagine why. At that time there were many plans for what seemed at first to be a huge pile of bricks, but when it came to the path round the brick bed, the pile had almost gone so the bricks were laid flat. One winter has shown me that bricks crack very easily in freezing temperatures—presumably the moisture content is greater over the larger area and this swells the brick so that it cracks—and that there are many kinds of bricks. Naive as this will appear to architects and builders, I had no idea that there were very heavy, hard ones; lighter, softer red ones; thinner yellow ones, and in my case, ones to which the old mortar stuck like glue. Things were not done in a slapdash manner in 1887.

Finally a one-brick outline edging bed was made at each side of the main pathway leading up to the brick bed, and into this went the old santolina bushes banished from the back of the conifer bank. This effectively trimmed down the Great Road, as one of my guests had rudely called it, to the dimensions of a Big Path, though the santolinas, like the macrocarpas mentioned earlier, were only to give an idea of the ultimate appearance of the path. Until they were there, I couldn't quite decide whether it should be stressed or blended away. In the event it is both, since in full sun the line blends into the grass because of the brilliance of light, and later on in the day shadows give it accent. Either way I am pleased because the santolinas, once straggly brown-based plants against which the cats used to like to sun themselves while delicately sniffing the scented air above them, have now taken well to their new catless environment and have bushed out—with a bit of help from my cropping occasionally— to a good little edging hedge. Because their bases were so bare, snow-in-summer was planted under them, in the hope that in time it would climb into the santolinas' lower branches as it used to climb the wire-netting cat-fence. This has happened to a certain extent, and the snow-in-summer (*Cerastium tomentosum*, I should say) provides a break in the hard brick edging which now only shows at intervals.

To prepare the third special bed the procedure was roughly as for the brick trough and the sink: sterilisation, rough drainage material, finer drainage material and then a good compost on top. This area was not so limited in size as the others, so the 6ft × 4ft inside the brick wall was sterilised with the flame wand first, then the next day given a soaking in Jeyes Fluid, together with the drainage material already lined up. As this was put in layer by layer, it was well covered with Jeyes Fluid, and finally filled in with a layer of thoroughly wetted peat. On top of that went sterilised compost. I was determined not to start with a weed problem even though eventually it would be impossible to dodge. Before that time came, however, I hoped that the plants planned for there would have effectively covered the ground. Since the irrepressible *Saponaria ocymoides* is one of these, the aim has now been more or less achieved, though the other plan for the use of the bed was, temporarily at least, as a nursery for my conifer seedlings. These were by no means ground cover, so that area has had to be kept clean by hand. Since this gives one an opportunity to examine the little plants no hardship is entailed, only pleasure in their progress and a determination to allow no competition for food and drink.

Big path, brick bed, conifer patch
new shed and view over rce hedge

The whole area—big path, brick bed, santolina edging and conifer plantation as it had by then become—was best seen from the box-room window. The admirable aerial view showed up the necessity for a backstop at the end of the big path—something to weld the path, brick bed and conifer patch together. After a long time of careful avoidance of nurseries on economic grounds, it was delightful to have a valid excuse to go again, so from the Stour Garden Centre run by chaps who really know about plants, as opposed to super-efficient salesmen, *Chamaecyparis glauca* 'Spek' came to grace the end of the mini-vista, with her magnificent 'skirts' of deep glaucous fan-like foliage held in overlapping layers, her head bent slightly as an acknowledgment of her change of circumstances. Now that she has been *in situ* for a year, she holds her head proudly higher, as much as to say, 'I've made it, you see!'

Obviously the next move to make the two gardens into one was to remove the stumbling block at the centre: those old tumbledown sheds with rusty corrugated iron roofs on which reposed the rubbish of many years—tin hats from the 1940s, cycle tyres, garden hose, odd bits of timber and all sorts of stuff, probably there as a weight to keep the 'tin' on. A daunting task of clearance. Inside was a stack of wood which came from the house when a party wall was knocked down. This was being preserved because I intended to build a smaller shed in a less obtrusive place, in which to keep some tools and equipment more appropriate to this side of the garden, saving quite a trek to get them from the existing sheds on the far side. Weighing up the jobs to be done, together with this major one, I decided demolition would have to wait.

While the last of the indoors work had been in train, many a glance out of the windows made the greatest garden worry at that time the lack of opportunity to deadhead the autumn flowering plants. Not only does deadheading conserve their energy for next year's blooms, but sometimes it even ensures bloom through three summers and two winters! But then, of course, the quality of the blooms gets steadily less. In this case there were some stocks which went on and on for this length of time, being carefully tended; even in snow there were blooms on them, and many more when the warmer weather came. Amazing.

Now that the garden is so full of lustily growing things, the easiest way to get round to deadhead is to take a peat bag, or one of those sheets of plastics with a handle at each corner, if I had one; though I suspect that these are more easily used spread out on a lawn while the owner deadheads the herbaceous border. The plastics sacks are practical and hold a great deal. I take two, one for weeds and one for deadheads, the latter going on to the compost heap. A wheelbarrow is impossible to get along some of my paths until the deadheading, tying back and trimming is done.

Deadheading is a worthwhile chore. Many of my less keen gardening friends think I am a fanatic about cutting off every single dead bloom, pinching out all the dead rhododendron and azalea blossoms (this is a long job on a prolific azalea like 'Mother's Day') and shearing over the heathers, aubrieta and thyme and so on. The fact remains, though, that by this practice energy, which would otherwise be directed towards seed formation, is conserved in the plant, so that, year after year, the perennials give of their best. Certainly bulbs left in the ground benefit to a great degree from this treatment, as well as from being allowed to keep their foliage until it is really yellow. The bulbs are then fed, ready for next spring, and they begin their period of dormancy.

Deadheading annuals is done largely to tidy the garden. Nothing looks more depressing than the sight of a lot of dead flower heads, especially after a summer storm or downpour of rain. It is also done to prevent the dissemination of unwanted seed. As we have seen, I was not quite quick enough off the mark in my first gardening year with three plants: poppies, honesty and balsam were to be found in drifts all round obstacles like tree trunks or scrubwood, as well as the isolated few seedlings which had probably been dropped by birds. But on the whole even I, the untidy, have fallen to and tidied up as a gesture towards plants which have given of their best and afforded so much pleasure with their blooming.

A number of plants tend to grow straggly unless some action is taken before they get too large. For most, it is enough to pinch out the growing tips of the longest shoots in order to give encouragement to the little lateral shoots to bush out the plant. My greatest difficulty is to distinguish between scrunched-up new growth and flower buds—that is, until the latter have taken a definite shape. Many a pelargonium has been wronged in this way, expected impatiently to flower while the stems grew longer and longer. For the first time, this year I have encouraged a unique pelargonium, possibly *P. graveolens* 'Madame Nonin', to flower. Previously it had straggled in a dusty mess about the office windowsill, but in the bright Suffolk light and an even temperature and with regular weekly care, at last I have a large bushy plant covered with tiny, pink, unspectacular flowers, streaked with purple-red. They may not look much but my delight in them is very noticeable.

To offset that bit of bigheadedness, confession must be made of my failure to nurture two lovely and expensive dwarf rhododendrons by not recognising that the mass of flower buds on them when they were planted should have been considerably reduced, to promote root growth. Now only a small portion of each plant is left and I shall have a hard time saving those.

Since the topic of pelargoniums arose with regard to deadheading, it might be appropriate to pursue it here, since in my blundering way several points have occurred during my growing of a number of varieties, which may be of interest. I was gratified to read recently that my automatic removal of dead flower heads and dead leaves was correct. I had been told that pelargoniums mildewed very quickly if kept too wet, and certainly my once-weekly method of watering seems adequate. But when they are put out in their pots, sunk to the rim in the brick bed for the summer months, a downpour can soon upset them; their blooms brown off and then rot.

In hot sun most varieties' leaves turn red, but this seems to do no harm although it looks alarming when they turn from a strong green to nearly crimson suddenly. In fact, my pelargoniums have a pretty tough time, so they must be tolerant plants. Sometimes outdoors the soil is dry, hard and burning hot, yet they flower on, though their performance is not so good as it might be under more favourable conditions of moisture and a good feed. Too much nitrogen makes for lush foliage and growth, but poor flowering, so they need a balanced diet, and room to breathe. One year I had so many cuttings growing on, that like the Old Woman Who Lived in a Shoe, I didn't know what to do for space. Eventually it was evident that growth was suffering and from the time that one lot were moved to another windowsill and others to another room, the plants picked up remarkably and were ready to be put outdoors after the frosts had gone.

With cuttings, the greatest threat to their well-being is stem rot due to overwatering. Now I find this quite inexplicable, since many of my cuttings have been successfully rooted in jars of water, where one would expect rot to set in immediately. They are potted up after a good root system has been established, usually within about four months.

On one of my nursery spending sprees, there were some irresistible dark-leaved dwarf pelargoniums with brilliant-red flowers, a combination that neither my mother nor I could pass by. We brought them home and subsequently identified them as zonal *P.* x *hortorum* 'Friesdorf'. Brought to London the plants, much to my dismay, showed signs of distress and before long appeared to be dying. Back they came to Suffolk and as it was summer, they went, with little hope in my heart for them, into a plunge bed. The very next weekend both plants were in flower again, and shortly afterwards cuttings taken earlier, in case both plants succumbed, flowered the same year.

Similarly two tiny pelargoniums given me by a friend in London because she had had them for a long time and they had made no progress, showed quite remarkable achievements here—in fact, when she saw them a few months later she had some difficulty in believing that they were the same plants. One was zonal *P.* x *hortorum* 'Fantasie', a very attractive double-white-flowered variety, and the other ivy-leaved *P. peltatum* 'Sugar Baby', which was so prolific that I spent nearly an hour on its welfare each Friday evening when I arrived. There was so much deadheading and deleafing to do to keep it tidy, and the trough of peat in which both plants lived on the sitting-room windowsill had to be kept constantly moist. Perhaps the even temperature from the storage heater had something to do with their progress.

Certainly all kinds of cuttings have prospered there, provided they are kept draught-free. Sheets of glass are used to lean against the windows where in winter time an icy breeze comes in. This seems to divert the airstream effectively from the plants while still allowing a change of air in the room. Seedling conifers have germinated there, and a shelf over the storage heater under the window in another room has proved an ideal place for keeping cacti in the manner to which they are accustomed. They actually flower now—delightful, crisp, elegant trumpets or daisy types of great delicacy of colour, some silvered or hairy, catching the bright light. But the spines often impale the unwary ladybirds who insist that they prefer conditions indoors to those outside, which is a pity because they are aphid-eaters.

The pots of all the indoor plants are sunk in troughs of peat which is wetted out each week. During the correct periods for each of the different kinds of cacti, water is given in the pot itself, carefully avoiding getting the plants too wet at the base, and so causing stem rot. This puts one on one's mettle regarding well-draining pots. The heater helps to prevent this rot too.

'Axminster'
regal pelargonium
from cutting

Chapter 14

Nearly Home

AS soon as opportunity offered, work on the new shed began. It was to be built from the old wood in the derelict sheds, but as before with the improvements made to the garage, new timber was used for the framework. The intention was to make as waterproof a job of it as possible, so that tools which were being stored in the house to avoid rusting could be kept outside.

Three very heavy 1887-vintage doors were to be used as the floor and these were laid on large timber baulks supported by bricks at intervals. I had thought a bit about putting a heavy mower into this shed instead of it taking up space in the garage, so it was vital to keep the floor level of the new shed as close to the outside ground as possible without incurring damp. No one wants to have to wrestle a great weight up even one step. Also I had had experience of stepwork with a handful of sharp tools, and had no wish to repeat it, so the 'foundations' were dug out of the ground to permit the underpinning and guess where the earth went—into the still sinking front path which was supposed to be lawn level by now.

The framework and flooring in position, tongued and grooved cladding was gradually taken off the old shed in the middle of the garden, cut down to size (thus removing the rotten ends), thoroughly creosoted and nailed on. This was somewhat haphazard (everything about this garden is) especially as I had decided to use part of the shed for keeping pelargoniums after their summer outing and therefore proposed to use three windows which had come out of the second half of the house. Two of these were to hang from their long edges from part of the new framework, while those in the front opened like ordinary casement windows. With my uncertain carpentry, and assisted by a second garden boy, Russell, this was achieved with a few odd gaps to be filled due, I like to think, to the off-square shape of the windows which had been made to fit the house.

The door of the old shed was then moved over and hung with the help of a friend who had just dropped in for a chat, and the shell was complete. Not until I moved from my London flat were the final touches applied. One weekend before the move, all the rubberised flooring was taken from the flat to provide internal wall-cladding and floor-covering. It took some time to do, but luckily the weather was kind and it was possible to roll out the material, measure up and cut it outside. Being pale-grey imitation wood grain, the lining looked in keeping with the rest of the exposed wood—and what a boon that dry, empty shed was when it came to the move the following week.

Previously painted 'tin' had been prepared for the roofing, and it was at this stage that the horrifying discovery was made that the framework of the shed was not square. So an interesting architectural feature of this building is a roof of four widths of corrugated iron each set at an angle to the front cross beam in order to line up with the side beams. How true that necessity is the mother of invention.

The new shed is tucked away near the hedge right on the edge of the new part of the garden, and is barely visible even in winter when the trees are leafless. One great advantage is that tools and equipment needed to develop and tame the new garden were more readily available than in the sheds on the opposite side of the old garden. Of course a waterbutt was fixed up to facilitate watering the new plants I proposed to put in, and a hose can be fixed to it if necessary. This was a great boon as the conifer plantation acquired new treasures.

Again temptation to visit nurseries was condoned by the requirement to make a good windbreak for the lower garden before the old sheds were demolished. Concurrently with the new shed-building—and in fact, long before, since all this was planned as soon as I had decided to take the second half of the house—a variety of conifers was chosen and some light relief from the necessary chores obtained by carefully siting each in relation to the others in terms of colour, shape, and ultimate height, as we have seen. Infilling with low-growing ground cover is a continuing process, though. At one stage I was worried about the spreading junipers and chamaecyparis, for fear they should be overcrowded with weeds which I simply had not the time to pull out. It was no good using Weedol in that case, as grass and nettles were growing right up through the centre of the plants. One day I just got right down to it, leaving everything else, cleared the whole patch for about the third or fourth time, and tried again with Ramrod. This time it worked for the whole season of weed growth, with only a few little stunted nettles trying to take over again. These were teased out with the minimum of soil disturbance and the surface closed over again. Ramrod contains simazine which forms a protective covering over the ground, which once disturbed, will of course allow weeds to grow. It is stupid to expect to plant in ground treated with simazine because it acts on vegetation as it emerges—or tries to—from the protecting cover. Several times I was caught out on this, but luckily not with an expensive specimen.

By now the old sheds were nearly demolished and my impatience to see what it would all look like when there was space there, urged me on to knock down the rest. In this Russell was invaluable and it must have worked off some destructive elements in both of us. The result was not surprising—just a big blank square of dusty, dry earth and a small square of concrete which was the floor to the old loo. Another challenge.

Having achieved two objectives in relation to sheds, and the rest of the garden by then crying out for attention, the mower went into action for the first and most difficult cut of the new season, and weeding revealed all sorts of invasive and encroaching horrors. Bindweed, that tiny-leaved unobtrusive menace which takes a stranglehold on the life of the nearest plants, was all over the place, and my lovely *Cedrus deodara* was shoulder high in grass, chickweed and speedwell, to say nothing of poppies and several of the dandelion family.

Then there were the transplanted chaps to be given more care. When the builders were trench-making, a change in the shape of beds near the brick trough at the end of the house was made. This partly came about at the time of the removal of the cat-fence and the shrubs along it. Now this hasty work had to be revised a bit, tidied up, weeded and the transplants fed. Also I had to take stock of the new wind conditions made by the removal of the sheltering shrubs and the opening out of new pathways. What a strange Topsy-type garden this is; but somehow it pleases with its extraordinary elements all wound about with pathways, odd steps and odder corners.

Thankfully all the transplants have made great progress. That often-moved red rose which started life in the bed outside the first back door, then escaped the builders by getting dug in under the back window, and has now been given an award of honour in the centre of the bed behind the brick trough, is once more in full bloom and covered with buds which carry its period of pleasure-giving right through to late autumn, very nearly five months. This is a bed which gets a lot of crosswind and I feared for that rose and other not so hardy subjects like *Daphne odora*, which is not at all sheltered. *Euphorbia wulfenii* hides behind the brick trough, and a *Hebe buxifolia* sits smugly behind the daphne. Fortunately during the previous winter, realising—just from putting my nose outside the new back door—how vicious the

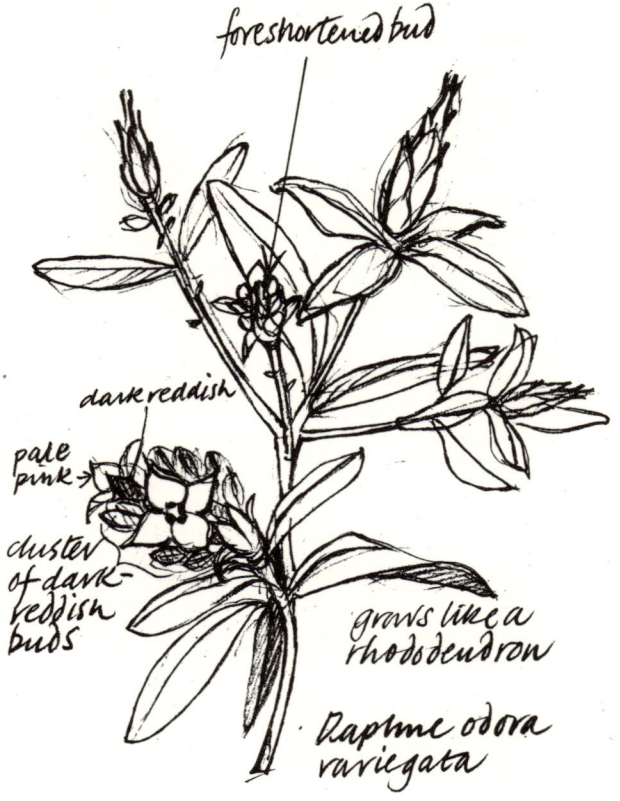

foreshortened bud

dark reddish

pale
pink →

cluster
of dark-
reddish
buds

grows like a
rhododendron

· Daphne odora
variegata

wind was on this side of the house as it plunged up alongside that all but blank wall and crashed through the available spaces, a netting shelter or windbreak had been erected between the house and that odd piece of privet hedge already described as having led to the old loo. This, together with other makeshift precautions, seems to have allowed the plants to re-establish in their new quarters without harm. *Leptospermum pubescens*, outside the netting screen, was given one of its own; two layers of wire netting with as much bracken foliage as could be mustered, sandwiched between. This gradually died down until in the spring it was only protecting the base, but as the plant's overall shining iridescence reassures me, it has come through unscathed, and even flowering.

Other shields have been hastily devised from roof slates broken by the gales, stood on end and pushed into the ground at a safe distance from the plant to avoid damage to roots. Open-paling gates, once discarded for burning, covered a gap where the wind whistled through; half a polythene and wire cloche bent round a small subject, with an opening on the lee side if it would not go right round, and indeed cloches themselves, if the plants allow, were useful. I am always seeking an excuse to buy a Stormcheat, a sort of wigwam-looking device which I am sure is wholly appropriate to this garden, but I never have the forethought to get it before the storm. The wire-netting rabbit barriers mentioned earlier in the book are in themselves some protection from the wind, but being so close to the plants they are not so effective as a more general barrier would be. One of the incalculable factors in erecting windshields on a sloping site is the distance actually shielded. On the flat, the wind is said to rush back to earth after lifting over a windbreak at a distance ten times the height of the obstacle. This may mean that if you are not careful, by protecting one part of the garden you are harming another, or even your neighbour's. On a slope, given the gradient, no doubt some mathematician could work out the equivalent to ten times the height of the obstacle, but I shall have to use the planting of expendable subjects as guinea pigs in experiments for various beds which are wind-harried.

This is, of course, the greatest single factor in planning the now-exposed old shed site. A few seedlings and cuttings have been put in pots sunk to the rims in the earth there, and these seem to be flourishing. *Cineraria maritima* is very good at resuscitating itself from a tiny cutting with a wisp of a root, and *Euphorbia wulfenii* is almost as tough, so by next spring there may be the beginnings of a shrubbery. The shed had been used for storing coal and there is quite a lot of it still in the earth there, so I pot-planted the more precious euphorbias as a safeguard, remembering what happened when I first planted out the paved garden where there was also coal.

Another consideration in the ultimate appearance of the old shed site is the existence of odd 'dots' of windbreaks: the length of privet hedge now turned into a topiary exercise, the row of plum trees and saplings, and the elderly philadelphus on the far side of the concrete loo base from the privet. None of these would be at all easy to dig up, nor would I want to do so as they protect the first garden so well. The problem is to find a formula for linking them which will not look too contrived.

The philadelphus, released from the one-sided bondage of the loo wall, stretched its arms luxuriously for the first time. After a good pruning, which it cannot have had for many years, next year it may well fill the gap, and the tub of miniature conifers covering the concrete at the moment can then be moved to be useful somewhere else. Winter jasmine also grows up with the philadelphus and no doubt this too will reach over and make friends with the bull, elephant, dragon or whatever the privet turns into under my far-from-skilled, clipping hands. So it seems that once more a wait-and-see policy will have to be adopted while other work gets done. There is plenty of this always, so waiting will be no hardship and will allow me to explore more possibilities than just another shrubbery.

If I were here often enough to tend it properly, perhaps a pool and fountain might be considered. On the whole I think this would be too sophisticated for the total concept, and too difficult to maintain with no assistance. There are a great many ornamental features which would give some point of interest to the site. Some are quite out of the question in terms of design and bad use of materials—plastics to simulate antique stone for instance —but it will be worth some research in that field. Conscious of increasing years, I am toying with the idea of making a series of raised beds before the area becomes covered with weeds. This appeals to me most in terms of easy gardening and the assurance that I shall still be able to do some even when I'm too old to dig and build sheds. The snag is that the plants would be in a very exposed position. Perhaps raised beds with frames weighed down with lead might be the answer—anything else would just blow away. I look with envy at the cold frames now advertised, with polystyrene bases and Perspex lights, and wish I had more time to keep the contents watered and the frames firmly on the ground. Wind!

Arches with climbing plants to bridge the gaps between the isolated bits of windbreak might also be considered. At last two or three clematises have grown up well, there is a pot of honeysuckle rooted from a cutting, and the winter jasmine all ready in position to clothe one archway. Each side of the house now has a proper framed gateway over which plants can be trained: the existing prolific honeysuckle already blooms extensively near the first back door; perhaps the rooted cutting of it should go beside the other gateway on the east side, risking the exposure and hoping for in-built hardiness. There are so many factors to be considered before putting up arches (for example, my maxim that tall things obscure views). The winter jasmine may long for something to let it get away from the philadelphus, but I do not feel like being hurried into a decision just yet.

Together with the old shed-site development, the existing bed alongside the privet must be taken into account as this lies just in front of the bald area. The leptospermum has established here, a *Spiraea* x *van houttei* is now a well-clothed shrub, having been properly pruned from its previous leggy growth, and the front of the bed is a mass of auriculas. Peonies of a beautiful deep red squat in front of the leptospermum, and at random intervals tall pale-blue flowered plants flourish all round the edges of the bed. Their incongruity for this position made me try to eradicate

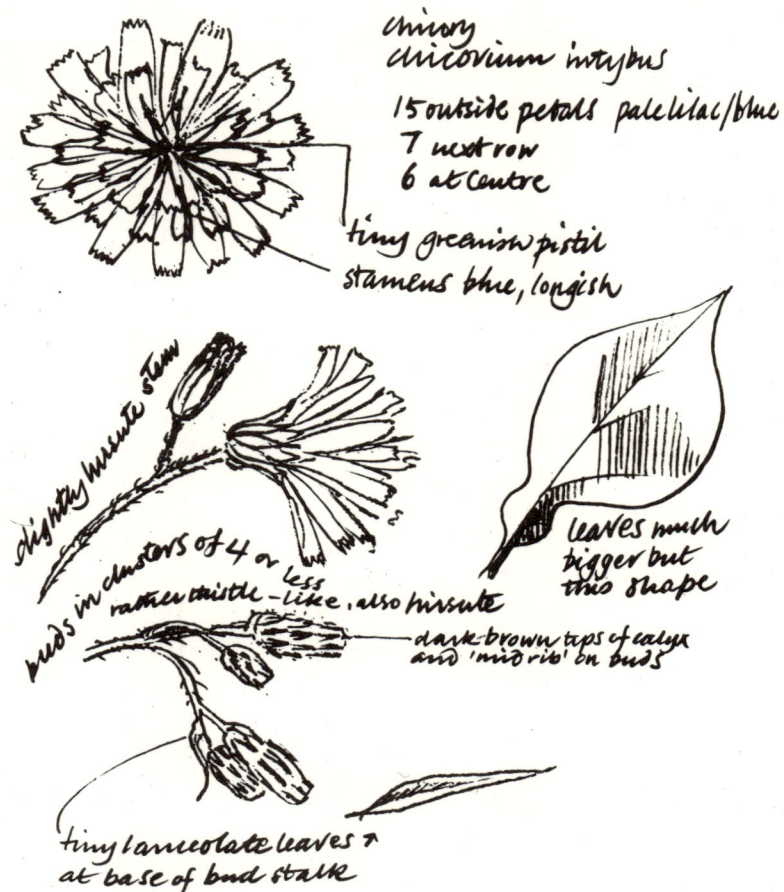

chicory
chicorium intybus

15 outside petals pale lilac/blue
7 next row
6 at centre

tiny greenish pistil
stamens blue, longish

slightly minute stem

buds in clusters of 4 or less
rather thistle-like, also hirsute

leaves much bigger but this shape

dark brown tips of calyx and 'mid rib' on buds

tiny lanceolate leaves at base of bud stalk

them all and this was no mean task, as their roots are like couch grass and wander on for miles, coming up with another tall stem some distance away. So far as I can tell they are chicory plants, but much as I like chicory, I am not prepared to tolerate their invasive nature, pretty though the flowers are.

The auriculas were the product of seed sown in a simple system called 'Pop-up pots'. As you can see from the illustration, these consist of two pieces, a stem which is filled with sand, and the top part which is filled with compost and the seed sown. Ideal for pelleted seed, which needs constant moisture to get going, it is equally right for auriculas which demand the same conditions. The stems of the pots are set into a wire frame, water is fed through the pots and into the pan beneath setting up capillary action, and a polythene hood placed over the lot, held high enough for the plants to develop by a plasticised wire strut at each end. The base of the hood, tucked in to return evaporated water to the pan, provides a constantly damp atmosphere. Before placing the hood in position, Captan powder was puffed over the pots to prevent mildew forming in these conditions of humidity. I was delighted with a 78 per cent germination from what is said to be very difficult seed to propagate.

Interest in auriculas was stimulated after a visit to another RHS show to see the dwarf conifers. I was now in a better position to resist these, and to turn my attention to another specialist field, since I had too many conifers already, I thought. The auriculas on show were quite phenomenal to a newcomer to their study. The attraction for me lay in the crispness of their marking, shape of flower and leaf, and their aloofness, rather like a cat's. This may sound fanciful, and odd coming from one who does not care for cats, but auriculas are in a world apart. The combination of colours due to careful crossing of one with another, leading to deep-purple blooms with a tiny white ridge at the edge of the corolla and a green edge to the petals, and leaves of a dark green-grey with a dusting of white powder on them, was to me quite extraordinarily fascinating. I had no interest in the method of achieving 'Green 3X' or 'The Rajah', only an overwhelming desire to possess a plant of that variety in order to look at it at leisure, to study it closely and perhaps to make a drawing of it.

That RHS show was somewhat expensive later, but seed was bought as well as plants. I had to wait some months before the plants were despatched, as it appeared not to be the season for sending out rooted offsets. When they arrived, they had magnificent roots and were in perfect condition. I began to be frightened of not being able to keep them this way.

It was unnecessary to worry: auriculas practically look after themselves, unless you want to show them. Their only demand is for good moist soil all the time, and those with farina or meal on their leaves, stems or flowers dislike getting wet as this blemishes the farina. As it was the mealy ones which attracted me in the main, the precious plants were kept indoors at first. They began to languish, to my horror. Now in a peat-filled trough outside in a spot which gets early morning sun but is shaded for most of the day until sunset, they have risen to their august feet, flowered, and grown offsets which will make more separate plants next season.

Three sources were tried for seed: Dobie's, Barnhaven and Mr Gordon Douglas. They were sown separately and carefully labelled, but as soon as the tiny seedlings were set out with their labels into a bed, the labels disappeared and I am now unsure where, for instance, that lovely nearly black one came from. The show made by these first-year seedlings was terrific and the planting-out distance proved to be correct for the increasing spread of foliage, although at the time it seemed sparse in the extreme.

Primula auricula frondosa made a delicate edging to the bed of alpine auriculas with their stronger colours. Frondosa is a pale lilac or cerise, with about fifteen tiny flowers to a truss, and much smaller than the others. Each of these was worth close examination, having some different feature or specially brilliant colour or texture. *Primula denticulata alba* was a superior present from the same donor as *Primula pulverulenta*, the latter giving immense heads of wine-coloured flowers in June.

From auriculas I feel it is a step downwards to polyanthus and the common primrose, but what glorious shows these make. From

Devonshire I was given a clump of lovely clear yellow primroses and these have bloomed and spread in a very satisfactory way. Giant polyanthus were seen on a stall in a local market. Much as I dislike the idea of aiming to make plants and vegetables grow to enormous size, these were most attractive because of their colour and I was then in need of something to fill a windowbox. Later the seed sown at the same time as the auricula seed developed into a mass of sturdy, brilliant-coloured blooms at the foot of the terrace-bed apple tree—just the right height above normal ground level to be seen and appreciated.

It seems most unlikely that I have come to the end of my sudden plant enthusiasms, but for the moment there is quite enough for one pair of hands to do. One encouraging event was to be awarded one of the many runners-up prizes in *Garden News*' Gardener of the Year competition after my third year as a gardener. The sack of fertiliser was put to good use in due season. As it was spread around, I wondered whether competitions and shows and cups and things are really won on a fair basis. Fertilisers, peat, insecticides and everything that enables the higher-income gardener to produce bigger and better flowers and vegetables, are surely beyond the means of old-age pensioners in these days of costly living, yet they are most likely to be the very people to whom a prize at a show would mean a lot.

Still, sitting ruminating over a meal and looking out on to a stand of sixteen red-hot pokers in full sun against the dark green of the privet hedge in shadow, with 3ft *Cineraria maritima* brilliant silver-white, and delicate abelia nearer the window, the sun picking up the gold of the spotted laurel and the yew on the terrace bed, I think there is much more personal satisfaction to be had out of successful gardening than can be won at any show. The areas which please me most are those where it has been possible to plan and plant uninhibited by anything previously on these sites—the conifer bank and the conifer windbreak plantation.

After six years' gardening at last I feel able to contemplate digging up thriving plants instead of being so thankful that something actually grows for me that I dare not dig it up. Some things are even expendable, and it is a triumphant moment as I leave a favourite nursery without having bought a single plant. Emancipation only comes with time and experience; of both I have little enough, but it is the prospect before us which lures every gardener onwards.

Bonuses are to be had from birds around the garden: the friendly robin who comes to watch me dig; the larks singing their hearts out on the wing; even the greedy blackbirds who fill the air with their song, and chatter in the tree tops when one is gathering soft fruit, saying 'There she goes, taking the food out of our mouths again', or grumbling as I gather the grasses straying into the flower beds, because I am taking away their cosy nesting material.

The sun sets in a blaze of glory, the afterglow luring one to continue working until the moment comes when tools have to be put away, with a torch held in the teeth, and darkness falls like a cloak over the hills. The silence is broken only at intervals by a pair of owls speaking to each other. Inside by the fire with tea and toast, future plans are drawn up. I dream on happily and drift into sleep. A cat-nap, did I hear someone murmur?

Bibliography

Anderson, E. B. *The Small Rock Garden* (1965).

Bates, H. E. *A Love of Flowers* (1971).

Bawden, Harold and Joan. *Woodland Plants and Sunlovers* (1970).

Bloom, Alan. *Alan Bloom's Selected Plants* (1968).

—— *Conifers in Your Garden* (1972).

Brookes, John. *Room Outside* (1969).

Coxhead, Elizabeth. *One Woman's Garden* (1971).

Cross, John. *Pelargoniums for All Purposes* (1965).

Field, Xenia. *Town and Roof Gardens* (1967).

Fish, Margery. *Carefree Gardening* (1966, last revised 1972).

—— *Gardening in the Shade* (1964, last revised 1972).

—— *Ground Cover Plants* (1964, last revised 1972).

—— *We Made a Garden* (1970).

Griffith, Anna N. *Collins' Guide to Alpines* (1964).

Hay, Roy (consultant ed.). *Gardening Year* (1968).

Hay, Roy and Synge, Patrick. *Dictionary of Garden Plants* (1969).

Heath, Royton E. *Rock Plants for Small Gardens* (1969).

Hecker, W. R. *Auriculas and Primroses* (1971).

Hellyer, A. G. L. *Shrubs in Colour* (1965, last revised 1972).

—— *The Amateur Gardener* (1948, last revised 1972).

—— *Your New Garden* (1935).

Lloyd, Christopher. *The Well-tempered Garden* (1970).

—— *Foliage Plants* (1973).

Martin, W. Keble. *Concise British Flora in Colour* (1965).

Oxford Book of Garden Flowers (1963, last revised 1972).

Park, Bertram. *Guide to Roses* (1956, last reprinted 1965).

Pearson, C. E. (ed.). *Complete Gardening* (1968).

—— *Everyday Gardening* (1968).

Phillips, C. E. Lucas. *Climbing Plants for Walls and Gardens* (1962).

Roper, Lanning. *Hardy Herbaceous Plants* (1960).

Sanders, T. W. *Encyclopaedia of Gardening* (1895, last revised 1966).

Stevenson, Violet. *The Weekend Gardener* (1966).

Thomas, Graham Stuart. *Climbing Roses—Old and New* (1965, last reprinted 1967).

—— *Plants for Ground Cover* (1970).

—— *Shrub Roses Today* (1962, last revised 1967).

—— *The Old Shrub Rose* (1955, last revised 1971).

Thrower, Percy. *Encyclopaedia of Gardening* (1962).

Underhill, Terry L. *Heaths and Heathers* (1971).

Underwood, Mrs Desmond. *Grey and Silver Plants* (1971).

Welch, H. J. *Dwarf Conifers—A Complete Guide* (1966).

Acknowledgements

My thanks are due to Professor and Mrs Bryan Brooke, without whose encouragement none of this would have happened.

Credits for photography are due to The Design Council for the photographs on pages   ,   and   ; to Mr L. R. Hite for that on page   ; to Duffin Containers Ltd, page   ; to Mouldcraft Products and to Studio Morgan. Aberdeen, page   ; and also to Henry Watson's Potteries and to the Buttermarket Studio, Ipswich.

Plant Index

Italic figures denote illustration

General Index

Italic figures denote illustration